STRENGTHENED
Developing the Leader Within

How to Connect with Your Vision, Discover Your Strengths,
Adapt Your Behaviors, and Achieve Your Goals

Copyright © 2021 Laura W. Miner

All rights reserved. No part of this publication may be reproduced, transmitted, or distributed in any form or by any means, electronic or mechanical, or stored in a database or retrieval system, without prior written permission from the publisher. Exceptions apply for "fair use", including brief excerpts or quotations referenced in published articles and reviews.

This book is designed to provide accurate, informative, and authoritative information with regard to the subject matter provided. The author of this book is not a licensed practitioner or medical professional and offers no diagnosis, treatment, or counseling. This book is not designed to be a definitive guide or to take the place of advice from a qualified professional. There is no guarantee that the methods suggested in this book will be successful. Thus, neither the publisher nor the author assumes liability for any losses that may be sustained by the use of the methods described in this book, and any such liability is hereby expressly disclaimed. In the event you use any of the information in this book for yourself, the author and the publisher assume no responsibility for your actions.

Paperback ISBN: 978-1-7364450-0-6
E-book ISBN: 978-1-7364450-1-3
Audiobook ISBN: 978-1-7364450-2-0

Dedication

To my incredible daughter, Taylor Ann. Thank you for continually inspiring me to model the way, shine bright, and be my best self.

To my amazing husband, Bill. Thank you for believing in me, encouraging me, and providing a pathway for me to pursue my dreams.

You two are my world. Always. In all ways.

Contents

Welcome 1

PART ONE: Connecting with Your Vision, Values, and Purpose

chapter one: Fueling Success with Science 7
chapter two: The Power of Vision 19
chapter three: Connecting with Your Vision, Values, and Purpose 45
chapter four: Stepping into Your Vision 61

PART TWO: Discovering Strengths and Adapting Behaviors

chapter five: Discovering Your Strengths 77
chapter six: Powering Success with Supportive Habits 91
chapter seven: The Experiment of You 119

PART THREE: Achieving Your Goals

chapter eight: The Art and Science of Goal Setting 133
chapter nine: Turning Vision into Reality 147
chapter ten: The Path to Mastery 163

APPENDICES:

appendix A: The Six Virtues and Their Respective Strengths 179
appendix B: The 24 Character Strengths 184
    Appreciation of Beauty & Excellence 185
    Bravery 189
    Creativity 193
    Curiosity 195
    Fairness 199

Forgiveness	203
Gratitude	207
Honesty	211
Hope	215
Humility	219
Humor	223
Judgment	227
Kindness	231
Leadership	235
Love	239
Love of Learning	243
Perseverance	247
Perspective	251
Prudence	255
Self-Regulation	259
Social Intelligence	263
Spirituality	267
Teamwork	271
Zest	275
References	279
Acknowledgments	289
About the Author	291
Share Your Opinion	295

Welcome

"Leadership is lifting a person's vision to high sights, the raising of a person's performance to a higher standard, the building of a personality beyond its normal limitations."

- Peter Drucker

Are great leaders born or made? Google this age-old question and you'll receive 369 million results for your reading pleasure. While passionate opinions fall across the spectrum and studies exist to support both sides of the debate, the truth is, it's not that simple.

Every one of us is born with innate leadership qualities, but this alone does not make one a leader. Frequently, these inherent characteristics go unnoticed and unacknowledged, quietly existing under the surface, waiting to be cultivated, nurtured, and developed. In other situations, one may be completely unaware of their individual traits and the true strength they hold in a leadership context, never embracing or elevating their potential. Further still, an individual may notice that their strengths amplify achievement in one environment but detract significantly under a different set of circumstances.

Thus, while each of us possess innate leadership qualities, developing and cultivating them is a required part of the equation. But what separates poor and average leaders from phenomenal ones? And how can we learn to evolve as leaders, parents, coaches, teachers, and role models for the benefit and betterment of those we influence?

Study the profiles of accomplished, highly regarded leaders and a few distinct commonalities arise.

Great leaders…

- have a concrete vision for the future and are well-versed at motivating others to embrace and support that vision.
- hold a clear set of values that guide their decision making and unwaveringly operate in alignment with those values, staying true to who they are at their core.
- focus on strengths over weaknesses, leveraging the power that emerges when individual strengths collectively collide.
- have supportive behaviors and habits that actively and continually contribute to their success.
- set actionable goals that line the path to their vision, making daily progress in the direction of those goals.
- never stop learning and growing, maintaining a perpetual commitment to their evolution and development.

Each of us possess a variety of leadership qualities that can be unlocked and unleashed to better serve our organizations and communities. By becoming STRENGTHENED, we can connect with those traits, embrace and develop the skills of great leaders, and create a ripple effect that makes a difference in the lives of those we touch. Developing the leader within unleashes our power to effect change and positively impact the world.

This book is written for those who understand the value of leadership and the importance of developing it. It's an invitation to develop the skills and traits that separate average leaders from exceptional ones. It's an opportunity to explore who you are and what you value so you can model the way for those around you. It's a doorway to becoming the type of leader who makes a positive difference in the lives of others.

Accepting this invitation requires work on your part. The pages of this book are lined with activities and exercises intentionally designed to take you on a thought-provoking, inquiry-based journey. At times, the exercises may feel heavy or difficult, and when they do, celebrate and embrace them whole heartedly. These feelings mean you are at the edge of your comfort zone where real growth and development take place - you are standing at the precipice of change.

Throughout this journey, I'll provide research-backed insights to help you understand the science behind the concepts, as well as stories from client experiences which serve to bring the concepts to life. In all cases, names and identifying details have been altered to protect client confidentiality, but the exercises embedded throughout the book are the same ones my clients used to achieve their positive results. If you commit to the process, positive results will follow.

One last thought before you begin…

As a leadership development coach and organizational consultant, I've written this book from a coaching perspective. It's purposefully designed to support your personal journey of developing the leader within. It rests on the framework of my signature leadership development program and involves a variety of psychological drivers to help support your success. I've tried to anticipate likely questions and address them throughout the book, but if at any point you have questions, comments, or feedback, I'd love to hear from you - you can reach me at hello@laurawminer.com. Depending on my travel and work schedule, it may take me a few days to get back to you, but I will personally respond.

With that, I'd like to officially welcome you to STRENGTHENED! It's time to develop the leader within.

part one

Connecting with Your Vision, Values, and Purpose

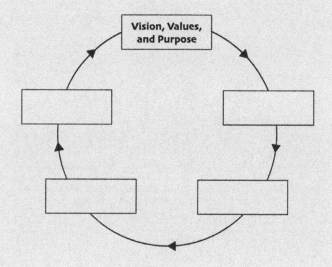

chapter one

Fueling Success with Science

"Your present circumstances don't determine where you can go; they merely determine where you start."

- Nido Qubein

Dane's Story

For years, feelings of frustration quietly nagged at Dane, leaving him with a sense of unease that consistently bubbled under the surface but couldn't be explained. He had a decent job, two adorable daughters, and took great pride in the co-parenting relationship he shared with his ex-wife. Yet, something felt amiss. Life certainly wasn't perfect - it had its fair share of ups and downs - but by all accounts, Dane lived a pretty decent life.

But was "pretty decent" *good enough*?

This nagging question badgered Dane like an unwanted robocall. He couldn't shake it; he couldn't avoid it. Over time, it grew more frequent, filling him with an unavoidable restlessness that had become visibly evident to those around him. Everyone had an opinion, but no one understood. Well-intentioned family and friends repeatedly told him he had a good life and should just appreciate it, but this wasn't an issue of gratitude for Dane. He loved his family, enjoyed his job, and appreciated the people around him, and still, he regularly felt unsettled and unfulfilled with life as a whole. Something was *missing*, but what that something was, was a mystery to him.

As Dane's 48th birthday approached, the weight of his frustrations gave way. As he put it, he was tired of "going through the motions and spinning his wheels". He wanted to escape the daunting feeling that he was "living a directionless life".

"In two years, I'll be 50 and if I don't dig into this now, I'm fearful my 50th will only bring more frustration and unrest. I don't want to feel drained like this anymore. I need to figure out why I'm not satiated by my good life, and I need to shake the guilt I feel when I think about wanting more. I just don't feel whole - I feel this sense of incompleteness that keeps tugging at me, but I don't know how to address it or make it stop."

I wish I could say Dane's feelings and frustrations were uncommon, but sadly, they're not. Going through the motions, day in and day out, is standard fare for many. But the good news is, it doesn't have to be. Research in the social, psychological, and leadership sciences has a lot to teach us about why people commonly feel unsettled and unfulfilled, and what steps can be taken to discover the reasons and overcome the hurdles.

But the question becomes… how do you integrate the vast amount of research into a systematic model that provides a framework for success *with* the flexibility required to accommodate individual nuance?

Welcome to STRENGTHENED: Developing the Leader Within!

As we step through the pages, activities and stories that follow, we'll explore research-backed insights that illuminate the path to success. We'll learn how others, including Dane (who we'll revisit in chapter nine), transformed their lives in meaningful ways by applying these lessons and developing the leader within. And most importantly, we'll *take action* to incorporate these insights into our own lives. But before we get too deep too fast, let's cover a few simple but critically important basics.

The Leadership Role

This may seem like a strange place to start, but it's important to address and acknowledge *who* is a leader. That moniker isn't solely relegated to those who hold formal leadership positions or carry certain titles. The grandmother who cares for her grandkids on the weekends is also a leader. The divorced couple who works in earnest to co-parent their children are leaders. The volunteer who lends his time to a youth sports organization is a leader.

Leadership is about who you are, what you do, and how you do it. It's not about the title you hold. As leadership expert Margaret Wheatley shares, "leadership is best thought of as a behavior, not a role".[1] It's about recognizing how your words and actions influence others while remaining mindfully aware of the ripple effect created by your decisions and doings. When positive leadership behaviors accompany formal titles, greatness can occur, but formal titles without positive leadership behaviors can lead to disaster.

While there are dozens of research-based leadership theories and countless books and programs that can be leveraged to learn them, this book is different. It does not espouse or champion a particular theory but rather, looks at the science behind developing the leader within. It takes a holistic approach toward who you are as a person and translates it to your role as a leader. It's a reminder, both in actions and words, that when you develop the leader within, you elevate yourself as well as those around you. And as the aphorism goes, a rising tide lifts all boats.

While innumerable seminars, certification programs, books, and courses focus on how to lead others, this book focuses first and foremost on how to lead one's self. It's drawn from extensive research, decades of experience, and recognizes that the best leaders 1) are clear about their vision and values, 2) acknowledge and use their top strengths, 3) consistently demonstrate supportive behaviors and habits, and 4) take goal-directed action on a perpetual basis.

A challenge has long existed, however, surrounding how to acquire and develop these "soft" skills which significantly impact the bigger picture. A common organizational practice is to take a great employee who excels in their particular role and promote them into a supervisory or management position. But being a good employee does not necessarily translate into being a great leader. As John Kotter, author, consultant, and leadership professor at Harvard Business School has shared, "Very few jobs in traditional hierarchal organizations provide the information and the experience needed to become a leader."[2]

Without training and development in the art and science of leading, individuals are left to their own devices, often producing results that pale in comparison to what *could be* if they were first taught how to develop the leader within. Whether one is trying to become a better little league coach, develop themselves as a more supportive sales manager, become a more influential executive leader, or anything in between, the process is all the same. It includes a continual practice of learning, developing, testing, and tweaking, all of which rest on a solid foundation of proven principles.

Fueling Success with Science

My personal journey through leadership development is not an uncommon or unique story. It began in my early twenties when I received my first leadership opportunity - one which was solely based on the fact that I was a good employee with a strong work ethic. There was no formal leadership training that took place; I simply learned by example. Thankfully, I had a wonderful example to follow, but this isn't always the case.

As time and opportunity unfolded, I found I had a natural passion and desire to evolve in my role as a leader. I took personal responsibility for my leadership development and began reading books, attending seminars, and implementing the practices and philosophies they touted. However, I repeatedly found that these practices didn't translate in the workplace. Was it just me? Was I doing something wrong?

It wasn't until the late 2000's, when I read a book called *The Leadership Challenge*, that a major a-ha occurred for me. While the books and seminars I had previously gravitated towards were highly rated in the popular press, they were primarily anecdotal. Their insights and instructions were generally based on the experience of a particular individual but didn't necessarily provide a predictable, repeatable process that others could successfully implement or follow. In other words, they weren't science-based or research-backed, they were simply one person's story of success. However, after happening upon *The Leadership Challenge* and learning how the equation changes when leadership principles are based on research and data, a massive shift occurred for me.

In my mid-40's, I put a thriving career on hold and made the decision to return to school and pursue a formal education in Organizational Psychology and Leadership Development. By contrasting my previous leadership experience with the data and research found in the social, psychological, and leadership sciences, I was able to move away from anecdotal accounts of how to lead and learn the predictable, repeatable patterns that drive sustainable leadership success.

Fueling success with science became my quest and helping others to bridge the gap between managing and leading became my purpose. As the research has shown, when our development is fueled with science, it naturally and intentionally leads to deeper self-awareness, which has proven to be one of the competencies that drive leadership success.[3]

But that's not to say this approach is easy. Simple? Yes! Easy? No. It requires time, effort, energy, and patience. There are no quick fixes for becoming a better leader and no magic pills to make it happen overnight. It's a process, not an event. But when you work through the process of developing the leader within, major shifts begin to occur.

The STRENGTHENED Success Cycle

What follows is a simple and flexible system that rests on a research-backed structure to help you connect with your vision, discover your strengths, adapt your behaviors, and achieve your goals. It provides the framework, accountability, and guidance to help you develop the leader within, while remaining flexible enough to adapt to your specific circumstances.

However, this book was not designed to be passively read and then set on a shelf. It's an action-oriented program, purposely crafted to help you get the results you seek. The words that line its pages provide valuable insights, but without action, those words quickly lose their power. To support your growth and development, exercises and assessments are woven throughout the book, taking you on a guided journey to develop the leader within. In addition, an accompanying workbook has been designed to further guide you through this process. You can download it by visiting http://lwm.link/workbook.

This book is separated into three parts. Here, in part one, we'll:

- Dive into the science and power of vision,
- Learn why having a clear vision is critical to success,
- Complete a few exercises to aid in crafting a vivid, compelling vision,
- Understand and identify the intersection of vision, values and purpose, and
- Learn about the mental models that hold people back from making their vision a reality.

In part two, we'll:

- Dive into the science of character strengths and take a psychometrically valid, science-based character strengths assessment,

- Discover how signature strengths propel personal and leadership success,
- Learn how to identify strengths in others as a tool of motivation and growth,
- Identify the habits and behaviors that bolster or block personal efforts, and
- Become our own experiment and identify the best practices that empower us to thrive.

In part three, we'll:

- Dive into the science and art of goal setting,
- Discover the psychological drivers that promote successful goal achievement,
- Leverage our vision, values, strengths, and habits to craft a comprehensive and actionable goal plan,
- Explore proven principles of personal mastery, and
- Conclude with a plan for ongoing growth and development.

This program is purpose-built to help you systematically develop the leader within, but it requires that you follow the process in a linear fashion, completing each exercise before moving onto the next section. If you do the work and follow the system, positive outcomes will follow. If you bounce around or skip sections, you'll miss important aspects that have been intentionally incorporated to act as psychological drivers that trigger intrinsic motivation, reflection, and growth.

As the adage goes, *how you do anything is how you do everything*. In other words, every decision made, word spoken, and action taken is actively creating the results and outcomes you experience. If you want a different tomorrow, you have to take intentional action today. If you want to leverage this program to truly develop the leader within, you have to follow the system.

As an aside... **The pathway to freedom is lined with systems.** Far too commonly, systems and structure are viewed as the enemy of freedom when, in fact, the opposite is true. Strong systems that rest on a foundation of supportive habits proactively enhance growth and development while empowering an individual to continually live into their best self. Failing to intentionally create systems does not mean systems aren't in place. Having no system is still a system - it's just one that leaves results up to chance. Change the system and you change the results.

This program is an intentionally designed system, but it's a component part, or a subsystem, of your bigger personal system. It enables you to get into the driver's seat and start looking at how your system operates so that you can evaluate what changes need to be made. Integrated throughout are the tools and methodologies for you to craft, create, and implement your own systems but nothing is one size fits all. Be your own experiment knowing that, where there's no inquiry or reflection, there's no ability to generate change.[4,5]

In *Thinking in Systems: A Primer*, Donella Meadows reminds us of the beautiful simplicity of systems, noting that they're nothing more than a group of elements connected by relationships and paired with a purpose.[6] When the purpose is clear, concrete goals and objectives can be created. As Sam Carpenter notes in *Work the System: The Simple Mechanics of Making More and Working Less*, it's critical to define your objectives, a process we'll walk through in great detail during this program.[7] Without clear objectives, decision-making is often aimless, leaving an individual incapable of effectively leading him or herself, let alone others.

It's also important to note that hard work doesn't automatically lead to success. Working really hard on unimportant or irrelevant tasks that aren't in support of your system will keep you locked in place. As conventional wisdom teaches, if you continue doing the same thing over and over, you'll keep getting the same results.

Systems change the results. They empower you to create a path to success that can be easily adjusted based on feedback from your actions and outcomes. Systems break you free from the chains of unpredictability that hold you back, helping you to achieve the results you're seeking.

Time to Dig In and Take Action

As we've established, information alone will not lead to growth, development, or change. The impact this book and program will have on your life and leadership skills depends entirely on your engagement with the words, exercises, and assessments that line its pages. But don't take my word for it, prove it to yourself!

One of the best methods for doing so is to evaluate yourself at the start of the program and again at the end, then compare the pre- and post-results. It's similar to having your body measurements taken before starting a new health and fitness program. If you begin the process knowing certain factors, such as your body fat percentage, muscle mass, and body circumference, then you can accurately assess whether those torture sessions at the gym are truly having a positive effect on your body. Additionally, being able to see the benefits in tangible, measurable ways drives motivation and enhances persistence[8], a phenomenon we'll explore further in part three.

On that basis, your next steps are:

- Download and/or print the accompanying workbook by visiting **http://lwm.link/workbook**.
- Visit **http://lwm.link/perma** for instructions on how to take the PERMA assessment, which measures human flourishing.

- Record your assessment scores in the space provided in your workbook. (This assessment will be taken again at the end of the program for comparison purposes.)
- Complete the 12-question self-assessment on page 3 of your workbook.

Success is not one-size-fits-all, but it does leave clues for us to follow. Take action, follow the clues, and you'll quickly find you create the necessary space to develop and unleash the leader within.

chapter two

The Power of Vision

"Without hope, without a dream, we start to move through life in a very hollow way."

- Richard Boyatzis

Steve's Story

Steve was exhausted, both physically and mentally. Every day felt like the one before, as he apathetically moved through life like a zombie with no conscious awareness. Day in and day out, it was always the same routine. Get up, get ready, go to work, go home, eat dinner, watch tv, go to bed, get up, and do it all over again. He was begrudgingly going through the motions of his 50-hour work week with little interest or joy in his endeavors.

It wasn't always this way, though. Steve used to love his job. A few years back, he was on the corporate fast track and had amassed a file chocked full of accolades and awards that highlighted his commitment to his team, demonstrated the care he extended to clients, and showcased the great pride he took in his leadership role. But after six years with the firm, the last three of which in the same role, Steve had lost his zeal. The organization's explosive growth had slowed, promotional opportunities were no longer readily available, and despite being in a great position, Steve was bored, lacked challenge, and had no thoughts or ideas for a different future.

Over time, his boredom morphed into a lack of engagement and his disinterest slowly crept beyond the corporate walls and into more personal areas of his life. He and his longtime girlfriend went their separate ways, he stopped working out and dropped his gym membership, and he was accepting fewer and fewer invitations to socialize and hang out with friends. The fiery passion he once held for life had dimmed to a faint flicker.

Though Steve's behavior was alienating him from others, Sarah, a business colleague and friend who had once worked for him, decided to reach out. She invited him to lunch and was thrilled when he accepted. It had been a few years since they'd spent any meaningful time together and she was excited for them to catch up. He'd been such a supportive and engaging boss, and she really appreciated how his efforts had shaped her growth and development. Though a friend had cautioned her that Steve wasn't the same man she once knew, Sarah found the rumors about his apathetic state difficult to believe.

That is, until she witnessed it first-hand. Where was the leader and man she once knew? And how could she remind him of whom he used to be and what he once stood for? She tried asking him about his dreams and goals, a practice he used to walk her through, but he was more focused on the past than on his future. And despite her attempts to revisit humorous and successful adventures from their past, much of their lunch was spent in flat, meaningless conversation. This was such a different experience for Sarah. Their conversations had always been a source of inspiration for her, but she was leaving lunch feeling discouraged and sad.

As she drove home, she couldn't stop thinking about how rudderless Steve seemed. He had no vision for his future and was adrift in a sea of discontent. Sarah didn't know how to help him personally but felt compelled to call Steve the following week regardless. She gently expressed how he seemed different, off, not the same go-getting, supportive, encouraging leader that she worked for years ago. Then, Sarah reminded Steve of a mutual colleague who had hired a business coach to help her reinvigorate her career.

Steve had forgotten about their colleague's experience but was genuinely interested in being reminded. The longer they chatted, the more Steve's interest in exploring his options grew, so Sarah offered to send Steve the name and number of the coach. Steve, acknowledging that he felt lost and needed direction, picked up the phone and gave me a call.

Steve was admittedly a bit lost. His early career goals had been achieved years before, but no new goals or aspirations had filled the void. He had fallen into a redundant rut and was unable to see that many of his frustrations could be alleviated if he had a renewed sense of purpose and a clear direction for this next phase of life. Without clear goals to guide his next steps, Steve would continue reactively responding to whatever life threw at him rather than proactively charting his own course. It was time to sail the winds of change and set a new course for the future.

Clarity is Strength

Imagine for a moment that you've hired a contractor to build your dream home. You tell the builder you want a 4,000 square foot house with five bedrooms, a large porch, and a three-car garage. You want the house to feel spacious and airy, and curb appeal is incredibly important to you. You let him know that you're eager to move in as soon as possible and, with that, the builder gets to work.

There's only one problem, *what will the end-result look like?* Will it be one story or two? Will it be a craftsman style or an English Tudor? Will there be a galley kitchen or a chef's kitchen? Will it have formal dining and living rooms, or an open floor plan where all living spaces flow together?

Without a well-crafted and clearly articulated vision, the likelihood of getting your dream home is slim to none. There are just too many variables. And the same is true of designing your dream career, ultimate business, or ideal life. If you don't define what the future looks like, you'll have little say in the end result.

A clearly articulated, compelling vision can open the door to new possibilities, transforming your life in the process.

As Peter Block shares in *Community: The Structure of Belonging*, vision is the deepest expression of what we want in life.[1] It's an invitation to possibility. You change your future by changing your thoughts, images, and conversations about that future. The future you declare and envision shapes who you are and what actions you take in the present.[2] And what you do today defines who you will become and what you will achieve tomorrow.

Your vision is an expression of who you are at your core. It's deeply connected to your dreams, values, purpose, and passion. It's what you seek to create and who you seek to become. And in the process of uncovering and defining your vision, you're empowered to turn your purpose into action.

Leadership experts James Kouzes and Barry Posner note in their phenomenal best-selling book, *The Leadership Challenge*, that in order for a vision to materialize, it has to speak to the head, heart, and hands.[3] In speaking to the head, it must be a logical vision that is just as easy for you to explain as it is for others to understand. This is true whether you're crafting a corporate vision that inspires a large team to action, or a personal vision that brings your personal dreams to fruition. If you can't easily share the essence of your vision, you may not yet have the clarity needed to bring it to life.

In order for your vision to connect with the heart, it must be passionately driven and emotionally compelling. Picturing your vision in your mind's eye should excite you to the very core of your being. It should speak to the whole of you - personally, professionally, relationally, and spiritually - filling you with a sense of completeness that reminds you daily that you're following the path that's meant for you.

Lastly, for your vision to connect with the hands, it must be actionable, empowering forward momentum on a perpetual basis. A clearly articulated vision provides the guardrails to bring your strengths, goals, behaviors, and actions into alignment. It creates a recipe for success that tells you which ingredients are necessary and helps you bridge the gap between dreaming and achieving.

The future you imagine is rooted in possibility. The minute you name your possibilities and connect them with your head, heart, and hands, they begin to take shape. Let's explore the research-backed insights that explain why this is the case.

As an aside... **Change begins with the questions you ask.** Questions allow us to pull back the layers and discover what truly lies at the core. It's about quality as well as quantity. It requires acknowledging that, all too often, the first question to surface is not the right question. Answer too quickly or without inquiring more deeply, and you may find yourself going down the wrong path or solving for the wrong problem. Fail to ask enough questions and the same challenges may plague you.

A simple technique for deepening your inquiry is to leverage "the five whys" methodology. Originally developed by Sakichi Toyoda of Japan, the approach requires repeatedly asking 'why' questions until you arrive at the root cause of your challenge, which generally occurs around five questions in.[4,5] As an example:

Problem: Our weekly online meetings are ineffective.

WHY? Because employees are multitasking.
WHY? Because they're disengaged.
WHY? Because the meetings aren't interactive.
WHY? Because the content is show and tell.
WHY? Because we didn't adjust the content or approach when we migrated from live to online meetings.

Solution: To identify ways of crafting exceptional experiences that heighten engagement and interaction.

The original framing of this problem led to finding fault with employee behavior - after all, they're the ones multitasking and not paying attention. Had action been taken on that initial response, the meetings would still be unproductive today. But as the layers were continually pulled back, each 'why' gets closer to the heart of the issue. Eventually, it surfaced that the real culprit was a failure to appropriately adapt the meeting's content and format after shifting from a live environment to an online format. Once this awareness surfaced, the problem was redefined and an enhanced solution for moving forward was implemented.

If you want to change the outcome, change the questions. Ask, then ask again differently, approaching every situation from multiple angles. If you do, the transformative power of questions and the deep insights they provide will amplify the results you see in business and life.

The Science of Vision

The power of vision is well-researched, but the practice of vision is severely underutilized. It's often talked about in theory but implemented by few. Yet, history shows us countless examples of companies and individuals who were able to achieve monumental feats because they crafted a detailed, vivid vision and then pursued it with unrelenting passion and persistence.

Thankfully, those success stories have left remarkable clues for others to follow. Take Walt Disney, as an example, and his famous mantra, "If you can dream it, you can do it".

The odds were stacked against Walt from the get-go. Born to a poor family headed by an ill-tempered, abusive father, the Disney household was shrouded in an oppressive air that left all four Disney boys eager to fly the coop and escape their father's violent temper.[6] Despite the harsh upbringing and years of undue criticism, Walt learned to dream big, focus on the positive, and never let the pain of his past darken the brightness of his future. He held a deep-seated belief that if you dream big dreams and consistently work at those dreams, anything is possible.

Walt wasn't alone in his beliefs. Decades of research and thousands of examples have shown the benefits of connecting with our dreams and creating a compelling, meaningful vision. But if this is the case, why don't more people take the time to do so?

I'll admit, I haven't always had one myself. I thought I did. It was my annual goal statement. But it wasn't a vision, nowhere close. Visions aren't about goals, at least not exclusively. True, they provide a powerful framework for identifying the goals that will bring your vision to fruition, but visions are far bigger and more compelling than a set of goals. They're aspirational, inspirational, and act as an energetic force that pulls you into your vision's orbit.

When you put pen to paper and start bringing a vivid vision to life, psychologically, your activation energy is being triggered.

The concept of activation energy originated in chemistry and speaks to the minimum amount of energy required for a reaction to occur. A good example of this can be seen in the process of lighting a match. The action begins with a quick, easy strike against the side of the box - that's the minimum amount of energy it takes to initiate the process. From there, a chemical reaction occurs that causes the match to flare up. The only difference when applying this concept to psychological processes is that we're referring to a practical mental model of activation energy. In other words, what's the minimal amount of energy required to launch an individual to action?

As it turns out, the act of capturing the vibrant, specific details of your future vision serves as activation energy. Once triggered, powerful reactions that pave the way to making the vision a reality are set into motion. This isn't magic, it's science! Let's explore why this is the case.

A Super-Highway to Your Future

This book and program begin with vision because, as the research has shown, having a clearly articulated vision primes important areas of the brain. It rewires who you are and who you're becoming and does so at the cellular level.

As the field of neuroscience has revealed, your thoughts and actions are continually changing the structure of your brain. When you repeatedly think about something or consistently take action in the direction of those thoughts, your brain changes its physical structure in response.[7] In other words, you're constantly wiring in and actively creating the person you're becoming. This is the process of neuroplasticity.

Think of your brain like a network of roads and freeways. Certain roads already exist and the cars, or recurrent thoughts, that travel these roads have well-established pathways they follow. As an example, if you had a pet you loved and adored as a child, then thinking about this pet may lead you down an ingrained path to happy memories and big smiles. This road, or neural pathway, is deeply forged and therefore the thought response is almost immediate. But let's say your first experience with a pet was being chased down and bitten by the neighbor's angry dog. The journey down this neural pathway will lead you to a very different set of memories and emotions.

However, just as the roads in our cities can be repaved or removed altogether, leaving nothing more than a faint memory of its previous existence, so too can the pathways in our brain. Our thoughts, and whatever we choose to repeatedly focus on, creates and reinforces our neural networks. In addition, new roads and highways can always be added.

Imagine that a new subdivision is being built and there are currently no roads leading in or out. Developers start by surveying the area before tilling the ground to create a conceptual space for the new road. Once they establish where the new road will be, they pack down the dirt, creating the initial pathway. However, it's not yet a road - it's just an idea - a dirt path that can't yet support consistent traffic. Navigating the road at this stage is a slow and deliberate process.

A series of additional procedures follow including laying a sub-base that stabilizes the pathway for the road, pouring a middle layer that provides support and protection against future damage caused by natural elements, and adding a binder layer that reinforces the roadway itself. After all those steps are complete, the final layer of asphalt is poured, and a roller truck ensures that the path is smooth and ready for a steady stream of traffic.

Multiple intentional steps are required to create a new road and ensure that it's primed and ready to support the upcoming patterns of traffic. And this same process happens in your brain when you're creating new pathways that lead you to your future vision. Initially, it'll be a slow and deliberate process but with time, repetition, and intentional effort, your new pathways will be securely forged. Before you know it, you're traveling on the super-highway to your vivid vision.

As these new neural pathways are developed and reinforced, it sparks a chain reaction that positively impacts efforts and energies in a variety of ways. In other words, as you work on your vision, your vision begins to work on you. But how can this be so?

The Baader-Meinhof Phenomenon

Have you ever thought about buying a new car and then suddenly, bam, you see that car everywhere? It's certainly not that those vehicles instantly flooded the streets the moment you decided to buy one, but rather, your awareness of the vehicle was heightened as it became a focal point in your thoughts. Maybe you've noticed the same thing happens when you start studying a new subject. Suddenly, examples of your new knowledge present themselves from every which direction.

This form of selective attention, also known as the frequency bias, activates our subconscious brain and draws our focus and awareness toward relevant images and information that always existed but previously remained in the background. You now see what you were once blind to. This phenomenon plays a large role in supporting achievement toward a clearly articulated vision as well. The moment you have a clear image of your desired future, the Baader-Meinhof phenomenon gets to work, bringing relevant examples, connections, ideas, and relationships to the foreground. Once they're in your awareness, you're in a position to act on them.

Don't mistake my words here. This isn't about simply thinking something into existence and poof, there it is. Bringing your vision to fruition requires hard work and consistent effort. But those efforts are aided at the subconscious level when you intentionally craft and connect with your vivid vision.

Goals

Goals are a critically important part of the vision implementation process, and we'll discuss them at length in chapters eight and nine, but it's important to note that goals are a means and not an end. Goals that exist in a vacuum, separate and apart from a larger vision, have been shown to produce *short-term* behavior change while lacking the emotional commitment necessary for long-term, sustained change to take effect.[8] Goals that lack a meaningful, emotional attachment to a bigger picture imbued with a deeper purpose often become goals for goals sake.

On the flip side, a meaningful goal that's deliberately designed to bring you another step closer to turning your vision into reality takes on a different quality. Infused with the power of your purposeful vision, goals become saturated with a level of intrinsic motivation that far exceeds the drivers of extrinsic motivation.[9,10] Our ability to strive harder and persist longer in the face of challenge increases significantly when our efforts are fueled by our aspirational pursuits.

Hope

As you'll learn in chapter five, hope is one of 24 character traits which researchers have discovered apply to all human beings, regardless of race, culture, socioeconomic status, or gender.[11] Researchers in the field of positive psychology have unitedly defined hope as "expecting the best in the future and working to achieve it; believing that a good future is something that can be brought about."[12] Hope and vision, therefore, share a symbiotic relationship; as you create and connect with your clearly articulated vision for the future, your hope in the future naturally begins to increase in response.

Why is this important? Research has shown that hope empowers people to broaden their thoughts and, in the process, increase the connections between their thoughts and their actions.[13] Simply put, they see more options and create more pathways for achieving their desired future state. In addition, research studies have shown that holding hope toward a future outcome increases perseverance while enhancing effective problem solving.[14]

Direction

It happens to the best of us. The workday kicks off in a bit of a fog with no clear direction as to what you'll do first. Before you realize it, it's lunch time and you haven't completed anything of material consequence. Sure, maybe you cleared your email, checked social media, and chatted with a colleague or two, but to what end did these activities move you closer to a meaningful, desired outcome? A vision inherently holds that much-needed end. It acts as your northern star, continually keeping you pointed in the direction of your goals and dreams.

Embedded within a compelling vision is a natural path for taking intentional action that's in alignment with your deliberate plan for the future. The clarity associated with the bigger picture helps eliminate the fogginess that can derail efforts and waste days. In this way, a radiant, detailed vision becomes the guardrails that keep you moving in the direction of your dreams and prevents you from getting too far off track. While this is admittedly a simplified explanation, its importance will grow as you navigate through the pages and practices in this book.

Developing a PEA Brain

Have you ever noticed how ideas and solutions naturally flow when you're in a happy mood, yet seem blocked when you're having a bad day? Embedded within us all is a set of psychophysiological states known as the positive emotional attractor (PEA) and the negative emotional attractor (NEA).[15] While both of these systems are important and the tension between these opposing yet complementary networks are required for success, maintaining an unequal balance that's more heavily weighted towards the PEA is a critical driver of achievement.

The PEA is the part of the system that helps us thrive. It sparks the default mode network (a neural network associated with social functioning and moral reasoning) and is characterized by positive emotions such as joy, interest, curiosity, amusement, and love.[16] When triggered, the PEA stimulates the parasympathetic nervous system, releasing positive hormones (such as oxytocin in women and vasopressin in men), and sparking optimism about the future, openness to new ideas and behaviors, and improved decision making.[17] These positive emotions have also been shown to release dopamine, the happy hormone, which contributes to cognitive flexibility[18], while also facilitating learning and enhancing creativity.[19]

The NEA, in contrast, is the part of the system that helps us survive. It's characterized by negative emotions, such as fear, anxiety, sadness, anger, and disgust.[20] These negative emotions are not bad in and of themselves. In fact, they are necessary emotions that steer us away from danger, letting us know when something is off kilter or out of sorts. The NEA is part of our warning system - it signals that there is something important to pay attention to.

In moderation, the NEA creates a necessary tension that benefits our growth and development. However, the NEA also triggers the sympathetic nervous system (SNS), which activates our stress response, releasing hormones such as cortisol while provoking our natural fight-or-flight reactions. When too much time is spent in an NEA state, it can trigger defense mechanisms while hindering learning and development.[21] The challenge is that negative events and emotions have been proven to be stronger than positive ones, a well-documented psychological phenomenon known as the "negativity bias". This is why maintaining an imbalanced ratio that keeps one anchored in the PEA three to six times more often than the NEA is so important.

An interesting and important finding is that the NEA can be triggered simply by *thinking* about a negative situation.[22] As an example, anticipating that an upcoming meeting with the head of another department will be contentious and combative will start to activate your SNS, releasing stress hormones and triggering your fight-or-flight response in the process. The anxiety associated with the assumed outcome will start to negatively impact you, even though the meeting hasn't yet occurred and no such outcome is guaranteed. The physiological response to negative thinking is a powerful force that can affect our health, relationships, and outcomes.

The good news is, there is an antidote to the negating effects of the NEA, and it lies in intentionally sparking the PEA. One of the ways we can do this is by anchoring ourselves in our vision for the future. Just five minutes devoted to envisioning your future can light up the PEA, tame the NEA, and help you keep your NEA/PEA balance in check.

Balance in Action

Failing to recognize when the NEA has its grips on us can lead to frustrations and setbacks, a lesson Jim knew all too well.

Jim was working on a deeply personal project. A series of traumatic events from his past had long been on his heart and he felt it was his life's calling to capture the devastating details and share them with others. His mind was ripe with ideas surrounding how he could use his past to improve other's futures, and he was eager to help those who had shared similar stories of pain with him over the years.

He had been working on the project for quite some time but was repeatedly frustrated by his inability to make the progress he sought. The biggest challenge was that, while the project was imbued with passion and aligned with his values and purpose, it was also emotionally heavy, consistently pulling him into a tornado of angst.

When he first began to tackle his project, Jim had created a solid set of structured goals that outlined a detailed writing schedule. But after a few weeks of attempting to follow his well-designed roadmap, he was emotionally overwhelmed. Sitting down to put his memories to paper flung the emotional floodgates wide open and feelings of sadness, anxiety, and anger consistently came rushing in. Most days he stopped before he started, failing to capture a single word on paper. And on those days when he did make progress, he felt drained and disgusted as if the dark cloud from his youth was hovering back above.

Despite the difficult emotions he was dealing with, Jim wasn't willing to let go of the project. He felt it was a part of his soul and his life's purpose. What he was looking for was a way to overcome the mental blocks that were preventing him from making deep progress on his life's work.

During our initial call, a pattern in his approach quickly surfaced. As he walked me through his thoughts and emotions surrounding his writing process, it was clear that he was anticipating negative emotions prior to hitting the first strike on the keyboard. This self-induced anxiousness was sparking a recurring cycle that ushered in his negative emotions and repeatedly caused him to freeze in his tracks without writing a word. His thoughts had his NEA working overtime, and the sympathetic nervous system was doing its part, sparking the natural flight response that was prompting Jim's procrastination.

I assured him, it's not you - it's human nature. It's how we're designed. And the good news is, when you understand the design, you can work *with* it instead of against it.

Over the next few weeks, Jim became his own experiment - an important process we'll discuss in detail in chapter seven. With a new awareness of the PEA and NEA, and the understanding that both are required in order to thrive and survive, we began exploring different ideas for shifting his personal balance.

After a bit of trial and error, Jim found his perfect equation. Working on his project was now limited to four days a week and never took place more than two days in a row. In addition, he limited himself to three hours each day (generally from 8 am - 11 am) and developed a specific schedule to deliberately impact his PEA:NEA ratio on those days.

He would begin his morning by reading his powerful vision statement, which elaborated on the benefits of his work and reminded him of the value his pain holds to serve others. Next, he wrote an intention for that day's writing and spent a few minutes meditating on the words and positive emotions behind it. Then, before sitting down to write, he listened to a three-song playlist that left him feeling positive, upbeat, and energized. With his PEA charged up and in full swing, he sat down, rolled up his sleeves, set the timer for 3-hours, and got to work.

When the timer rang, the first thing he did was get out of his chair, crank the tunes, and listen to his upbeat playlist once again. This created a quick jolt to his PEA and immediately started counterbalancing the three hours that were just spent in an NEA state. In addition, on his four writing days, he pre-scheduled calls with positive-minded friends and colleagues as a means of intentionally crafting additional PEA events that would take place on the heels of his writing sessions. Realizing that the outdoors sparked his PEA and left him feeling refreshed, he also began spending his writing-day lunch hours eating outdoors while watching light-hearted videos on YouTube, another PEA-inducing habit.

Jim's new and balanced approach to his writing left him invigorated and excited, producing massive results in a short period of time. He was able to finish the book and is now in the process of sharing his message with non-profit organizations who support the same audience. He turned his childhood *mess* into his *message* and is positively impacting the lives of others, just as he had dreamed of doing.

Prior to our sessions, Jim was letting his NEA control him. It was getting between him and his dreams and creating barriers that prevented success. Once Jim understood the neuroscience behind this psychophysiological system, his world shifted. He took control of his NEA by intentionally sparking his PEA and leveraged the necessary tension between the two to drive success.

Uncovering Your Vision

Now that we have an understanding of the critically important role that vision plays, and we're aware of the science that underpins its impact and fuels our success, it's time to connect with our personal visions and bring them to life.

For most of us, our vision already exists. It lies in our passions, is embedded in our values, and if we look closely enough, we'll see evidence of it all throughout our lives. Our job is to look for the patterns, connect with the insights, and bring our vivid vision to the forefront of our thoughts. Admittedly, this isn't always easy or intuitive, but through a few intentional exercises, we can begin to uncover the clues that bring our vision into focus.

For me, my passion for positively improving and enhancing workplace cultures first surfaced in 1991. I was 19 years old and happenstance put me in a physical location where I overheard frustrations flowing from my organization's weekly management meeting. They were voicing challenges surrounding morale and interdepartmental teamwork but failing to explore possible solutions. Instinctively, ideas started feverishly exploding in my mind like Jiffy Pop on the open fire on movie night. As I began scribbling these ideas down, more and more continued to flow, resulting in a long list that I was overwhelmingly excited by.

Some days later, unable to shake my optimism toward an improved environment, an opportunity arose to share a few of those ideas with my then-current boss. She was open to my insights, appreciative of my efforts, and responded by telling me to craft an implementation plan, which I eagerly dove into with full force. Nearly thirty years later, I can still remember how invigorated my soul felt to work on solutions that would improve our workplace culture while positively impacting the livelihoods of our employees. In that moment, the seeds that would eventually shape my vision and purpose were planted.

When I submitted my proposal, I fully expected that she and the management team would review my suggestions and then possibly, maybe, if I was lucky, find value in an idea or two. I left the proposal in her inbox as instructed, and then waited for what felt like months – though in reality, it was only a few days. Not only was the vast majority of my proposal met with praise, but much to my surprise, I was put in charge of the new initiative. I was given the support needed to succeed, the space required to learn and work through various challenges, and an opportunity to scratch the surface of a passion that would eventually become my life's work.

When we reflect on our past and intentionally seek out those times in our lives when our interests were sparked, we often find that elements of our dreams and passions were sitting there in plain sight all along, just waiting to be discovered. Sometimes the clues are found in the books we're drawn to, the volunteer opportunities we seek, the conversations we get excited about, or the subjects we choose to study further. Themes emerge from the emotions and excitement of our past, and a path unfolds unearthing our vision for the future.

Let's do a little digging and begin exploring that path.

⇒ **Exercise #1**: Below is a list of 25 questions designed to help you identify recurrent themes that exist in your life. These questions are also outlined on page 4 of your downloadable workbook, along with room to answer and explore each question. The trick here is not to overthink the answers but to give yourself the space to explore whatever naturally surfaces for you. If a question doesn't fit, skip it. If another question is worthy of multiple answers, give it the time and reflection it deserves. We'll use the answers to help shape exercise #2, so be sure to record your answers in writing.

1. What types of books or magazines do you read?
2. What are the subject matters of your favorite podcasts?
3. If you're surfing the web, what article topics grab your attention and pull you in?
4. What type of content is featured on the social media accounts you follow?
5. What do others say are your natural strengths?
6. What common feedback do you receive from others?
7. What skills come naturally and easily to you?
8. What types of activities do you love to do?
9. What are some areas of interest where, once you start, you get so immersed in the activity that you lose track of time?
10. Are there any workplace or community challenges that you have a passion for solving?

11. What topics get you so excited that you can talk about them for hours?
12. If you won the lottery and didn't have to work, what would you do with your time?
13. What fills you with excitement and joy?
14. If someone asked you to teach a class tomorrow, what subject would you teach?
15. Is there a theme that has repeatedly surfaced over the span of your life, drawing your interest each time?
16. What are five things you want to do or achieve in your lifetime?
17. Are there any activities you enjoy today, that you also enjoyed as a child? How does engaging in these make you feel?
18. If you could spend the day with anyone, dead or alive, past or present, who would it be and why?
19. If your schedule was completely clear tomorrow and you could spend the day doing whatever you wanted, how would you spend it and why?
20. What are three subjects you would love to learn more about?
21. In looking back over your career, what was your favorite job or role and what did you love about it?
22. If you could go back to school and earn any degree, what would you pursue and why?
23. If you could spend the next week volunteering your time to a worthy cause or initiative, who would you support and why?
24. What daily or weekly tasks or activities do you wish you could spend more time doing?
25. List five things that make you happy and bring an immediate smile to your face?

⇒ **Exercise #2**: Read through your answers from exercise one. As you do, look for patterns to emerge surrounding passions and themes that repeatedly arise for you. Perhaps you see that a love of learning consistently surfaces. Or maybe there's evidence of a particular activity that repeatedly captivates your thoughts and attention. Possibly you find yourself continually drawn to a certain subject or towards supporting a specific cause. The answers can be far and wide and will be different for everyone but connecting with the unique themes that routinely surface can act as a gateway to discovering your passions and crafting a compelling, clearly articulated vision.

With these connections and insights in mind, close your eyes, set a timer for ten minutes, and imagine it's ten years from now. Your efforts have all paid off and you're living your ideal life, thriving in every way imaginable. Each and every day is the expression of what you had always hoped it would be and the life you've created fills you with energy, meaning, and purpose.

What does your ideal life look like? Where do you live? Who are you with? What kind of lifestyle are you enjoying? What does your career look like? What kind of work-life balance do you enjoy? How do you spend your time? How is your health and fitness? What are your spiritual practices? Are you actively involved in community? What impact are you having on others? What legacy are you building that will continue on after you're gone?

Imagine every area of your life and do so with great detail. *Feel* what it's like to be living your ideal life. The more vividly you imagine it, the more powerfully you'll spark your PEA and the quicker your neural networks will begin to make new connections.

When the timer is up, grab your workbook and turn to page 9. As you reflect on the ideal life you've just envisioned, repeatedly complete the statement, "In my ideal life, I _____".

Capture the range of free-flowing ideas and images that played themselves out in your mind. The more detailed and specific, the better. Don't overthink it or censor yourself, just write down what came to mind when you took a detailed look at your life 10 years from now. This is the beginning of your vivid vision.

As a quick side note, everyone's journey is different. As an example, if you're currently focused on building a business, feel free to change the prompt to: "In my ideal business, I_____". Remember, this program is about you and your future. While it's built on a research-backed, science-based foundation, it's also intentionally designed to flexibly adapt to your unique needs.

⇒ **Exercise #3**: Sit for a moment, reflecting on your "Ideal Life" responses and thinking about the various goals, dreams, aspirations, and desires that surfaced in the process. As you look at each statement, assign a category label to the left of the statement. Some sample categories might include career, relationships, finances, physical health, emotional health, spirituality, recreation, community/social, personal growth, and physical environment.

Once each statement is assigned to a category, you'll be ready to start crafting the first draft of your vision statement.

Crafting Your Vision… Take One

Vision guides the path we follow. It helps define our purpose and goals and provides guardrails for decision-making that keeps us moving in the direction of our dreams. Without clearly articulating a compelling vision, it's far too easy to succumb to the Groundhog Day effect, falling into the mundane trap that plagued Steve at the beginning of this chapter. But with a meaningful, detailed vision in place, you can chart a clear path to a purposeful future.

On that basis, the journey you are about to embark on is one that will produce a first draft of your vision. Some may find that this initial attempt supports their dreams in a vibrant, motivating, action-oriented way, and others may get to chapter three (where we'll revisit vision through the filter of values) and realize it needs some tweaks or adjustments. Regardless of the path you find yourself on, it's important to realize that your first vision is not your last vision, nor must it be worthy of a Pulitzer prize. You get to make as many adjustments and alterations as you want until it speaks to the future you're ready to proudly and confidently step into.

In addition, version done is always better than version none so don't allow perfection to stand in the way of completion. Get your first draft written, celebrate the success of having done so, and then revise as needed. In the process of doing so, you're sparking your PEA, making space for the Baader-Meinhof phenomenon to take effect, deepening your strength of hope, and igniting your motivation. This is fueling success with science.

Before you begin writing, I want to share five tips for crafting a compelling, meaningful vision. By incorporating these aspects into your first draft, you'll find your vivid vision begins to naturally take shape in a powerfully supportive way.

1. Make it vivid, specific, and detailed. Your vision is a picture in the form of words that speaks to your head, heart, and hands. The more detailed it is, the more power it has to act as a catalyst to change. Research across several fields has affirmed that our words create our worlds. We move in the direction of the images we envision, the conversations we hold, and the texts we read.[23] As thoughts translate into action, positive outcomes follow. This is why visualization is standard practice in the field of sports psychology. As one research study showed, basketball players who spent 50% of their practice time visualizing a perfect free throw consistently outperformed those who practiced shooting the ball 100% of the time.[24] But it all starts with a vivid, specific, and detailed vision of what you want your future to hold. There's no set number of pages or rigid framework to follow. It's just you, envisioning your amazing future, seeing the details come to life, and connecting with the emotions as your ideal life unfolds on paper before your eyes.

2. Anchor it in the future. The future-oriented nature of a vision is far more important than is often realized. As the research has shown, constructing a clear and compelling image of your future affects the thoughts, ideas, and feelings you hold in the present.[25] Your attitudes and abilities shift in response to the vision you hold, further developing your hope and optimism in the process.[26] When you possess a clearly articulated vision and revisit it regularly, you set the wheels in motion for where you're going *and* who you'll be when you get there. This is an important aspect that's often overlooked. Your vision isn't just about what you're working to achieve, it's also about who you're becoming in the process, a concept we'll explore in more detail in chapter 3. How far out in the future should your vision be anchored? There's a bit of flexibility here depending on your life stage and aspirations, but 5 - 10 years is ideal. Far enough out that you have the time and space needed to bring your aspirational vision to fruition, but not so far out that you lose sight of what it is or why it matters.

3. Check that it challenges you. If your vision doesn't push you out of your comfort zone and challenge you to grow more, learn more, and become more, ask yourself if you've truly captured its full essence. Endeavors that require you to learn new skills, develop additional competencies, and expand your knowledge and awareness will actively promote self-efficacy while increasing perseverance in the face of obstacles.[27] Big, challenging visions motivate elevated effort in the pursuit of aspirations. However, small visions that rest comfortably within the boundaries of one's comfort zone often fade into the background having been weighed down by boredom and disinterest. This is why it's important to remember that if your vision doesn't scare you *at least a little* you may need to revisit it.

4. Confirm it's based on a growth mindset. A growth mindset rests on a foundation of believing that who you are and what you're capable of can be cultivated through your own intentional efforts.[28] It's the difference between someone who feels stuck with the hand they were dealt and someone who uses that hand as a starting point. A hallmark of those with a growth mindset is their willingness to push through obstacles, reframing failures as learning opportunities, and turning setbacks into successes.[29] Those with a growth mindset are able to dismiss judgment while increasing resiliency, knowing they're on a path to discovery that will include feedback in the form of obstacles; a process that's empowering to growth minded individuals because it paves the way to making that future vision a reality.

5. Ensure that it's inspiring. A vision naturally and organically inspires action when there's an emotional connection to the purposeful future you're creating. When you start to *feel* the excitement and enthusiasm surrounding the vivid details of your vision, such as who you're becoming, what you're achieving, the impact you're making, and the lifestyle you're enjoying, intrinsic motivation deepens, hope is sparked, and optimism builds. Details transform a plain vision into a vivid vision, imbuing it with the passion that makes it compelling. When you are truly moved by your vision, you'll move mountains to achieve it.

⇒ **Exercise #4**: Picture your future like a jigsaw puzzle; your vision is the image on the front of the box. With this clear image before you, you can arrange the pieces and assemble the puzzle. However, without a clear image depicting the end result, putting together the puzzle is a serious challenge.

A meaningful, compelling vision takes time to craft. Rarely does it flow from the mind to the hand to paper in quick succession. It takes dedicated time and deliberate effort to capture the vivid, moving details of your future vision. Knowing this, set yourself up for success by turning off your phone and notifications before beginning, hanging a do-not-disturb sign if necessary, and giving yourself a few solid hours of distraction-free time to get lost in the process.

The good news is, you've already done much of the work. The questions you answered, the statements you completed, and the categories you assigned to your "Ideal Life" exercise have brought your themes and passions to the surface. They've helped you identify what's most important to you and they've begun shaping the details of your future. Writing your draft vision statement is simply a matter of bringing it all together.

As a last reminder, remember that when it comes to writing your draft, done is better than perfect. Vision statements are an ever-changing, ever-evolving, living thing - *just as you are* - and you'll revise and adjust your vision as time goes on, including again in chapter three.

With that, it's time to start creating your compelling, detailed vision for the future. Some prefer to capture this digitally, while others enjoy the process of physically writing it out. Either way, space has been provided on pages 11 - 12 of your workbook to craft your vivid vision. Are you ready to fuel your success with science, spark your activation energy, and anchor yourself in the PEA? Let's begin!

chapter three

Connecting With Your Vision, Values, and Purpose

"It's not where you've been, it's where you choose to go next, that counts.
It's not who you've been; it's who you decide to become—and that changes the story you're about to live."

- Shad Helmstetter, Ph.D.

Before we dive into chapter three, I want to take a quick moment to applaud you. The difference between wishing for a different future and creating one lies in the choices we make and the actions we take. To Dr. Helmstetter's point above, choice changes our story. The deliberate choice to act on the exercises in this program and, in the process, to decide where you're going and who you're becoming, is the first step to bringing your vision to life.

While visions don't magically materialize overnight - and intentional, deliberate effort awaits you in the journey ahead - continued and consistent action in the direction of your dreams will produce significant results. It's been repeatedly proven that when vision and values collide with action, greatness erupts with significant force. I'm excited for the future you're creating and the rewards your intentional efforts will bring.

Vision and Values in Action

In 1982, Johnson & Johnson faced an unfathomable crisis when seven consumers died in the Chicago area from cyanide-laced Tylenol purchases. Panic quickly spread across the U.S., the company's market share plummeted overnight, and many feared this heart-breaking catastrophe would mark the end of the nearly 100-year-old organization. Johnson & Johnson knew they had to take swift action, but how do you respond quickly when there's no playbook to reference? In 1982 it was incredibly rare for companies to have just-in-case crisis plans waiting in the wings, forcing then CEO, James Burke, to look for guidance in other ways.

Thankfully, the path forward had been captured and clearly articulated in 1943 by General Robert Wood Johnson, the company's third president and a member of the founding family.[1] Though the company was nearly 60 years old at that point, Johnson sought to capture the essence of its history and the values it was founded on prior to their ensuing status as a publicly traded company. The document he penned, which came to be known as the "Company Credo", served as the organization's moral compass. It provided a values-based framework for decision-making which outlined the priorities and responsibilities Johnson & Johnson had to their customers, employees, communities, and stockholders, in that order.[2]

As Johnson & Johnson's website shares, their credo challenges the company to always put the needs and well-being of the people they serve above everything else.[3] It calls for the leaders to consistently take just and ethical actions, to recognize that their first responsibility is to the users of their products and services, to provide employees with a sense of fulfillment and purpose in their jobs, to be responsible to the communities they live and work in, and to be good citizens to the world community as a whole. These values gave Burke the direction needed to craft an action plan in response to the 1982 crisis that prioritized people, health, and safety over corporate profits.

To the dismay of various stockholders and some members of the board and leadership team, Burke elected to recall all 31 million bottles of Tylenol in the United States while also rolling out an expensive tamper-resistant packaging initiative. While some voiced concern that such efforts could bring financial ruin to the organization, Burke knew these actions were necessary in order to save lives, protect consumers, safeguard jobs, and preserve the brand. As it turned out, the development of tamper-resistant packaging not only became the tool that rebuilt Johnson & Johnson's trust with the global community, but it also had far-reaching impacts that positively enhanced the packaging standards across a wide variety of industries.

Burke's decision-making was guided by Johnson & Johnson's credo and the clearly articulated vision and values embedded within. The Credo provided a framework for moving forward, empowering the organization to emerge stronger than before. Had this framework and the company's strong connection to their vision and values not existed, the outcome may have differed significantly.

One can never know for certain what challenges or obstacles lay ahead, but with a clear vision steeped in values, the roadmap for overcoming them lays at your fingertips.

Your Vision and Values

With the first draft of your vision complete, the next step is to gain clarity on your values and ensure that your vision and values are in alignment.

Values are the foundation that our lives are built upon. A strong foundation will support the weight placed upon it, but a weak foundation will develop cracks over time until it finally crumbles. When we have clarity surrounding our most important values, everything else filters through these values and decision-making becomes a more natural process. However, when the values we hold and the priority we give them are not explicitly outlined and understood, it can significantly exacerbate the challenges we face.

Let me illustrate with a personal story. When I was in my 30's, my professional vision included securing a regional management position that provided significant income as well as the flexibility to work from home and/or according to my own schedule. Embedded in this vision were two specific goals: 1) to increase my income so I could provide my daughter with more opportunities and experiences, and 2) to schedule my work responsibilities around my role as a parent.

Within a year of articulating this vision and taking action to network with others who could expose me to such opportunities, I received a phone call that would forever alter the trajectory of my life. Within 24 hours of that phone call, I was on a plane to Las Vegas interviewing for my dream job and experiencing a whirlwind of activity that was truly intoxicating.

I was wined and dined by a team of well-dressed, articulate executives, put up in a luxury suite at a high-end resort hotel, treated to an amazing meal where multiple bottles of wine were free flowing for hours, and sold on the myriad of perks that would accompany my role. This was it, my dream job, I was certain! The opportunity met both my goals, so I eagerly signed on the dotted line without giving much consideration to anything else.

Boy, was that a huge mistake! I didn't take the time to investigate the backstory of the executive team, or interview their top clients to see how they were perceived in the industry, or explore if they had a vision, mission, and values that I would be proud to represent. As time and circumstance would eventually expose, the company's ethics and my personal values were not in alignment.

Slowly over time, like the parable of the boiling frog who doesn't realize the water is too hot until it's too late, the stress of working for a morally corrupt company whose expectations compromised my personal code of conduct began to take its toll. The cognitive dissonance was affecting my physical health, impacting my ability to be a present parent, and wreaking havoc on my mental game. Every day I was torn between what was ethically right for my clients, and the unprincipled expectations placed on me by my organization. There was no middle ground and I felt completely out of alignment. It wasn't until I got clear on who I was and what I stood for that my life changed.

My deep reflections taught me about the value I place on honesty, integrity, and honoring a common good that considers all stakeholders within a system, not just stockholders. I learned that I had an inherent drive to defend those who didn't have the knowledge, information, or insights to defend themselves. I uncovered the priority I place on a supportive environment that encourages learning, development, and growth. I discovered that I absolutely had to find my voice and act from my own ethical position, or I would never be whole. And finally, I came to understand the importance of guarding my values as I moved forward in life.

Perhaps most importantly, I realized that if I had been clear on my values *prior* to catching that flight to Vegas, I never would've accepted the job. The writing was already on the wall and the red flags were flying full mast; failing to see and acknowledge what I was signing up for was fully on me.

Whether we're concretely aware of them or not, we all hold certain values dear, which impact every area of our lives. These impacts can be positive when we live in accordance and alignment with our values, or substantially negative when they are in opposition. But it all starts with identifying the core values that shape our lives and ensuring they're truly *ours* and not based on the expectations of others.

This brings up an inherent challenge - frequently, our values are not necessarily our own. They're the extension, and sometimes the expectation, placed on us by others. Maybe our parents instilled in us that family is the most important value. Or perhaps our spouse or partner placed an expectation for us to adopt love as our highest priority. Or maybe we work in an environment that dictates that the company's core values become our own, regardless of whether they're in alignment with our personal code of conduct or not.

If our values are misaligned, or if we've never truly identified or introspected on them, it can have severe consequences on our health, our relationships, and our general well-being. You may be wondering, if values are this critical, why didn't we address them before we created the initial draft of our vision?

Personal experience, formal education, and countless interactions with companies and clients in a variety of industries have taught me a critically important lesson. Simultaneously contrasting values against past experiences *and* future expectations is one of the most powerful ways to truly connect with them. After all, it's easy to *say* you hold a particular value but far more difficult to live into it when faced with a decision that places two important values in conflict with one another.

Uncovering Your Core Values

Before we uncover, define, and connect with our core values, it's important to clarify exactly what values are. The dictionary defines them as, "a person's principles or standards of behavior; one's judgment of what is important in life". In practice, our values reflect our needs, wants, and desires, serving as a driving force in who we are and what we stand for. They shape our priorities and act as a filter in decision-making. Living authentically into them can lead to a life full of joy, fulfillment, and satisfaction. However, a lack of clarity surrounding values can lead to confusion, conflict, and discontent. Identifying the values that are core and central to who we are as individuals is paramount to living wholly.

Luckily, the process for doing so is both simple and rewarding. Beginning on page 13 of your workbook, you'll find a 7-step method that walks you through the process of uncovering and prioritizing your values. In addition, a comprehensive list of values has also been included to assist with your exploration.

Before you dive in, there's one more important note to mention. Our values, and the ranked priority they hold, can change over time so it's important to regularly review and revise as needed. As an example, when I became an empty nester and active parenting was no longer part of my daily routine, I was able to elevate and re-prioritize my values toward education and lifelong learning. These were always important to me, but previously they fell below my value of parenting. Once my daughter was successfully launched into adulthood, I reorganized my priorities and returned to school to pursue a formal education.

The best way to keep your thumb on the pulse of your values is to keep your list readily available and review it every 90-days. This gives you an opportunity to assess what's changing or shifting in your life and to make any necessary adjustments. Often, it's not the values themselves that change, but simply the priority that's assigned to them. Ask yourself, what are the values you now need to prioritize in order to achieve your vivid vision and become your future self?

⇒ **Exercise #1**: It's time to find out by turning to page 13 of your workbook and diving into "Seven Steps to Uncovering and Prioritizing Your Values".

Where Vision, Values and Purpose Collide

Far too many people live lives of anxiety and boredom. They long for a different pattern to life, craving better outcomes, yet waking up each day doing the same thing as the day before. They become mired in habitual patterns that hold them back instead of developing habits and behaviors that propel them forward.

This was the dilemma that plagued Steve, whom we met at the beginning of chapter two. He had grown unhappy, bored, discontent, yet he didn't have a vision for restyling his future. Without a vision, he lacked a connection to purpose, and without purpose, he lacked the impetus to change his course. Like Bill Murray's character in *Groundhog Day*, Steve's life felt hopelessly redundant. It wasn't until Steve went through the processes I'm sharing throughout the pages of this book that he began to see the path to a brighter future.

After exploring the questions in chapter two, reflecting on how his answers shaped his ideal life, and connecting with the themes and patterns that reignited his hope, excitement, interest, and joy, Steve began developing a compelling, detailed vision for his future. The exploration tapped into his natural talent for mentoring others, provided a pathway for growth, and empowered him to get involved in a leadership program that focused on developing leadership skills in students at the local community college. In the course of mentoring and teaching others, he experienced tremendous growth himself, and the spark he once held began to shine bright yet again.

But an interesting lesson surfaced for Steve in the process. His previous downward spiral had been accompanied by a deep-seated belief that he wasn't born for greatness. In his mind, he was just an average guy living an average life and there was no greater purpose he was meant to pursue. Steve's fixed-mindset had him believing that purpose had to be big, bold, and capable of changing the world in remarkable ways. He failed to see how his personal passions and interests held the powerful potential to positively impact young leaders within his community.

Steve's view of purpose as a "bigger than life" construct is not uncommon. Purpose, and the role it plays in our lives, is frequently misunderstood. It's often made to be much larger and loftier than it ought to be, but why is this the case?

The messages portrayed in the movies we watch and the human-interest stories we read often illustrates purpose as a special gift bestowed by a higher power on a select few. This misconception paints a picture that purpose strikes like a bolt of lightning and stays with you for life. No effort, no energy on your part - just BAM! Purpose struck! Now you have it and you always will. After all,

- Mother Theresa was born to serve the poor;
- Gandhi was born to free India from British rule and inspire civil rights movements across the globe;
- Martin Luther King Jr. was born to bring awareness to racial inequality and right the injustices directed toward people of color; and
- Greta Thunberg was born to elevate discussions, initiatives, and responses addressing the existential crisis arising from climate change.

And while true, it may happen this way on rare occasion for a lucky few, most everyone else follows a different path. Most of us embark on a journey to *discover* our purpose. As notable psychologists from Yale and Stanford revealed, you don't find your passion and purpose, you *develop* it.[4] It doesn't passively happen upon you, you proactively happen upon it. It's an act of exploration that uncovers naturally engaging patterns and themes and is followed by deliberate action to take the exploration even further. Your intentional choices and actions breathe life into your purpose, empowering your purpose to then drive additional choices and actions, creating a powerful feedback loop that reinforces the exploration and pursuit of your purpose.

Purpose is embedded in the vivid vision you hold for the future and is amplified by the core values that shape who you are. Where vision, values, and purpose collide is where your motivation to eagerly greet each day with vigor and zest emanates from. This collision stokes the fire of your calling, your meaning, your why. Where vision, values, and purpose collide is the source of wholeness that empowers you to thrive fully, live intentionally, and make a difference in the lives of those around you.

You don't have to be Mother Theresa or Gandhi to have purpose. It's not set aside for the MLK's or Greta Thunberg's of the world. Purpose comes in all shapes and sizes from the ER nurse who takes great pride in keeping his patients as calm and comfortable as possible, to the college professor who seeks to have genuine connections with her students, to the flight attendant who just wants to consistently add smiles to passengers' days. Purpose is the fuel that sets a soul on fire and inspires intentional, meaningful, affirming action.

The Science of Purpose

Is it really *that* important to connect with your purpose and discover your why? According to a wide breadth of science-backed research, the answer is a resounding yes.

Dr. Majid Fotuhi, MD, Ph.D., and the author of *Boost Your Brain,* reports that "having a purpose in life is one of the most important factors for protecting your brain against cognitive aging."[5] As his research revealed, people with a high 'Purpose in Life' score were 2.5 times more likely to stay cognitively sharp in their 70's and 80's compared with those who had a low score. In addition, researchers at Rush University Medical Center in Chicago found that individuals who scored high on 'Purpose in Life' cut their risk for developing Alzheimer's disease by half.[6]

Further research from Johns Hopkins University showed that elderly participants who acted on their passion for mentoring students in public schools, and who did so for a span of two years, improved their cognitive performance while showing a measurable increase in brain volume in the areas responsible for memory and learning.[7]

Additional research findings revealed that having a purpose in life positively impacts physical health and well-being. Researchers studied more than 7,000 participants, aged 50 and older, over a six-year period of time. The results demonstrated that those participants who felt they had a purpose in life were more proactive in getting routine health care check-ups, made healthier lifestyle choices, and spent 17% fewer nights in the hospital than those without a sense of purpose.[8] In other words, those who actively lived according to their purpose were intrinsically motivated to proactively take better care of their health, a move that also resulted in substantial savings on health care costs over time.

A strong purpose affects every aspect of life, guiding individuals, businesses, organizations, and movements to more meaningful achievements. It drives intrinsic motivation, promotes engagement and fulfillment, and contributes to improved health and well-being. It sorts the meaningful from the meaningless, while actively engaging and energizing efforts. Purpose puts you on the path to living with intention and fills you with the sense that what you do matters.

However, connecting with your purpose does *not* mean rainbows and unicorns suddenly appear. The journey takes work. Opportunities for learning and development appear in the form of setbacks and hurdles, and it's only in pushing through these challenges that real growth occurs. When this happens, take a moment to be grateful and celebrate, knowing that success lies at the edge of your comfort zone.

Unlocking Your Purpose

Unlocking your purpose is a *process* of self-awareness, not a one-time event. It's an evolution where nothing is wasted. Every action, every step, every misstep, can contribute to your purpose if you intentionally look for the lessons, identify the patterns, and uncover the themes. Most everything is built on something already in existence, but frequently large, grandiose expectations of what purpose *should* be leave us blind to what it actually *is*.

Hints of purpose are often sprinkled throughout one's life, though admittedly, it can be easy to miss, or even ignore, the signposts along the way. My purpose bubbled under the surface for more than 25 years. It nagged at me consistently, quietly at first, then louder and louder as time went on. It wasn't until I was in my 40's that it finally demanded my attention, refusing to be ignored any longer. I suppose you could say I was hit upside the head with a proverbial frying pan.

For me, the final straw came after repeatedly facing the same workplace challenge with numerous clients and organizations. The pattern went like this: I'd be hired as a sales and marketing consultant to drive revenue for a company, only to quickly realize that many of the challenges they faced were systemically driven by a fractured company culture. The culture, which was set and/or endorsed by those at the top, wasn't an area that was open for discussion with a sales and marketing consultant and any attempts to address the larger, more pressing issues were swiftly stopped in their tracks.

Improving workplace cultures through organizational change has been a repeated theme in my life since my earliest beginnings in corporate America. It dictated the books I read, the workshops I attended, and the magazines I subscribed to. But it took two and a half decades before I fully recognized that this was more than curiosity, this was my passion and purpose in life. And with that, I made the decision to pursue a Master's in Organizational Development and Leadership, followed by a doctorate in Leadership Studies, which I'm actively pursuing at the time of this writing.

While it was never my intention to return to school at this point in life, my purpose and calling had grown too loud to ignore. It was no longer quietly bubbling under the surface; it had become all consuming. I *knew* pursuing this path was what I *needed* to do. And once I began taking action to respond to its calling, everything else began falling into place.

Has your purpose been trying to get your attention? Has it been tugging on your shirt tails, trying to get you to take notice? The process of uncovering your purpose isn't always easy but the rewards for doing so far exceed the effort.

Thinking back on the exercises you've completed thus far, what are the themes that have repeatedly surfaced throughout your life? Is there a nagging feeling, an unanswered question, or an ongoing curiosity that has captured your attention for years, or perhaps even decades? Is there an area of interest that consistently spans across different areas of your life? Where do these connections and commonalities come together and what messages are embedded?

When Steve reflected more deeply on his answers, he suddenly realized his passion for mentoring and developing others had been a consistent theme since early adulthood. He recounted stories from his teenage years of being a youth summer camp counselor and the tremendous sense of joy that erupted from that experience. He spoke of the excitement he felt when he worked for a company who required that each employee spend one workday per month volunteering at the local Girls and Boys Club. And he suddenly realized that his favorite movies over the years - Star Wars, Dead Poet's Society, and Finding Forrester - all shared a common thread of characters who demonstrated strong mentorship qualities. Moments sprinkled throughout his life made him realize, his purpose was always there, it was just waiting for him to take note.

Are there any passions or interests in life that you haven't fully acknowledged or embraced? Has your purpose been knocking on the door with no answer?

⇒ **Exercise #2**: Turn to page 20 in your workbook and explore the questions provided for "Uncovering Your Purpose". Take note of the patterns that have repeatedly surfaced, the emotions they provoke, and the role you want them to play in your life going forward.

Crafting Your Vision… Take Two

With exercise #2 complete, contrast your responses with the initial draft version of your vision and consider the following questions:

- Are the themes and patterns you identified woven throughout your initial vision statement?
- Did you find that some aspects were included but others were inadvertently left out? If so, explore why this may have been the case.
- Does your vision go deep enough, or do you need to incorporate your themes with more detail and thoroughness?

Now reflect on the fit between your values and your vision statement.

- Does your initial vision statement fully reflect the values you hold most dear?
- Are there any aspects of your vision that are in conflict or at odds with the priority ranking you assigned to your values?
- Are there aspects of your vision that need to be revised in order to be in full alignment with your values?

As we reach the end of this chapter, it's nearly time to revisit and revise your vision statement. Before you do, I have two additional tips for writing a compelling, meaningful vision.

1. Make it vivid, specific and detailed.
2. Anchor it in the future.
3. Check that it challenges you.
4. Confirm it's based on a growth mindset.
5. Ensure that it's inspiring.

6. Align it with your core values. When core values and vision are misaligned, the NEA is triggered making it more difficult to achieve the desired future state associated with the vivid vision.[9] When this misalignment occurs, conflicting attitudes, beliefs, and behaviors surface, acting as roadblocks to success. Values remain abstract and ambivalent until a conscious decision is made to imbue life, actions, and the possibility for a new future with the power they hold. A vision that's steeped in values and aligned with who you are at your core viscerally supports growth and development, propelling you toward your future vision.

7. Infuse it with the passion of your purpose. Don't compare *your* purpose to another's and don't measure yourself by someone else's yardstick. You are unique and how you bring your purpose to life will be distinctly your own. When purpose is uncovered and embraced, and your vivid vision is infused with the power of your purpose, you're empowered to live a more meaningful life while reaping the benefits associated with improved health, enhanced well-being, and greater cognition. Purpose acts as a motivational spark that calls you to action, bolstering perseverance in the face of challenge.

As previously mentioned, some may find their initial vision is spot-on, already encompassing their values, elevating their purpose, and exciting them to the very core of their being. However, for most of us, we may want to explore some revisions based on the exercises completed since the initial draft was written. If you find yourself in the latter camp, take your time with the process and give yourself the space and freedom to enjoy the exercise. Space for doing so has been provided on page 21 of your workbook. Remember, a meaningful, compelling vision that speaks to your heart and calls you to action will change your life in significant ways, creating a ripple effect that positively impacts the lives of those you touch.

chapter four

Stepping Into Your Vision

"Don't tell me the sky's the limit when there are footprints on the moon."

- Paul Brandt

What Stands Between You and Your Vision?

A compelling, vivid vision opens the door to possibility and creates a pathway to success. It lifts the ceiling from dreams and extends an invitation to follow a purposeful path toward an intentional future. It sparks the PEA, drives motivation, inspires hope, contributes positively to health and wellbeing, and empowers the Baader-Meinhof phenomenon to bring relevant opportunities and insights to our awareness.

Yet, if it's fundamentally known that humans thrive when they have direction, and if it's understood that vision, values, and purpose provide that much-needed sense of direction, *what holds people back from developing a clearly articulated vision and pursuing it with gusto?*

While the answers will vary from person to person, there are seven common challenges that frequently contribute to the gap between one's present circumstances and their future vision. Any one of these challenges on their own can create a barrier to success, but when multiple challenges are stacked upon one another, the journey can become increasingly difficult. Thankfully, understanding these potential landmines and learning how to navigate around them can shrink the distance between where we are and where we're headed.

Let's explore the top seven challenges that most commonly hold people back.

1. Muddy Waters. A murky vision will consistently yield murky results. It's only when a vision is specific, detailed, and compelling that it will capture the heart, inspire the soul, and come to life in the mind's eye. A clearly articulated vision eliminates haphazard decision making and makes space for intentional, purpose-driven action to become the norm. The possibility for a better tomorrow is rooted in the clarity of today. Ask yourself, is your vision crystal clear or are there still some muddy aspects that need to be flushed out?

2. Expecting Perfection. Don't let expectations of a perfect vision hold you back from taking action. Version done is always better than version none and there are no rules stating that a vision can't continually be updated as you travel the path toward achievement. If you're feeling held back by the fact that it's not "quite right", give yourself the gift of experimentation as you begin to test it out. If you find aspects that sounded better in theory than practice, adjust accordingly. All visions evolve over time so don't hold yourself to an unrealistic standard of what it should be out of the gate.

3. Lack of Intention. Some people daydream about a different future but fail to put in the effort to bring it to fruition. They write a vision statement only to stuff it in a drawer, continuing all the while to live on autopilot. Their actions and behaviors don't change, instead, they continue reactively responding to what life presents without proactively looking for ways to alter it. Tomorrow's vision is determined by today's actions. A vivid vision fueled by intention will propel one in the direction of their future goals and dreams. Ask yourself, is your intentional effort in alignment with your desires for the future?

4. Welcoming Distractions. Every one of us gets 24-hours each day, but how we spend it is of individual choice. Bringing a vivid vision to life takes time, effort, energy, and a consistent focus on sorting priorities. How important is your vision *really*? Is it more important than watching TV at night? Is it worth getting up an hour earlier each morning? Is it worthy of less time on social media or turning off notifications for a few hours? Only you can decide, but the choices you make will determine if and when your vision becomes a reality.

5. Competing Responsibilities. Sometimes, obligations associated with other responsibilities can fool us into believing that pursuing our vision would be selfish or irresponsible. This commonly happens when we have other people in our lives, such as a partner, kids, or elderly family members, who rely on our support, leaving us feeling that we can't rock the boat or risk the paycheck. However, pursuing a meaningful vision does not mean you have to burn the boat. Visions can materialize in smaller steps, as long as consistent action is taken in the direction of your dreams.

6. Too 'Whatever'. Believing you are too old, too late, too established in your career, too busy, too (insert excuse here), will ensure that you are, in fact, too 'whatever'. These excuses, which are commonly fueled by fear, protect us from failure while simultaneously preventing success. They keep us in lockstep with the status quo while our dreams quietly fade away into oblivion, only to resurface as regrets later in life. What if Colonel Sanders had decided that, at age 62, he was too old to franchise the chicken recipe he'd spent decades perfecting?

7. Listening to Others. If you share your vision with someone and they don't react as positively as you'd hoped, this is not a reflection of your vision; it's a reflection of that person. We all know that change is hard, but sometimes we forget it can be more difficult for those around us who fear how our changes may potentially impact them. If your vision speaks to your heart, hands, and head, and inspires you to action, don't second guess yourself and don't change the vision, change who you share it with.

These seven challenges are not as simplistic as they may initially seem. A simple challenge would be coming home from work to find a large tree branch blocking your driveway but being able to drag it off to the side and still park your car. Simple challenges tend to have obvious, simple solutions. However, the seven challenges above represent belief systems, or "mental models", which influence our behaviors and actions at a much deeper level.

Mental Models

A mental model is a shortcut for how we perceive, process, and react to the world around us. Mental models consist of the images, beliefs, and stories we hold that shape the conclusions we draw and the perceptions we adopt. These important heuristics allow us to develop go-to methods for processing repeat information so we can move quickly and efficiently through the massive amounts of inputs received in a given day.

Imagine if each and every time you saw a stop sign, you had to mentally process what the message was telling you before taking action. The time delay created by this process would have ongoing ill consequences, potentially leading to catastrophic results. The mental model you hold for stop signs allows you to react quickly and consistently without having to consciously process what the meaning of a stop sign is.

While this is a simplistic example, mental models are a complex framework that affect every aspect of decision making, often at unconscious levels. Though these models may save us time on the front end, they can equally prompt additional challenges on the back end, as was the case for James and Bryan.

As a leadership development coach, I was hired by their CEO to work with James, the sales manager, and to evaluate the challenges that seemed to be limiting the team's growth and development. As I quickly learned, James and Bryan, the top producing sales representative, had a toxic, combative relationship and the tension between them was affecting the cohesion of the team as a whole.

In my conversations with James, I learned that the issues stemmed from Bryan's arrogance and entitlement. As James explained, Bryan felt his "top producer" status should excuse him from certain responsibilities, such as having to participate in sales meetings or submit reports in a timely fashion. Understandably, James' vantage point left him increasingly frustrated with Bryan, broadening the chasm between them.

When I met with Bryan however, I learned that James lacked the same level of experience as Bryan yet consistently found it necessary to micromanage him. James checked in on him incessantly, negatively impacting Bryan's productivity and causing him to be less responsive to James' ongoing barrage of communications. Bryan's frustration was bubbling over and unfortunately, he wore his irritation on his sleeve.

Deeper conversations revealed that both men held blame-oriented mental models, which only deepened the discord between them.

As is often the case, viewing the world through mental models leaves space for our shortcuts to become assumptions that prioritize our perspectives above, and sometimes to the exclusion of, anyone else's. James assumed this was an issue of entitlement because his mental models led him to process the late reports and missed meetings as intentional acts of defiance, which he attributed to prima-donna behaviors. But the assumptions drawn from his mental models were incomplete and inaccurate.

In reality, the late reports were because Bryan had more paperwork to process than anyone else. He was consistently struggling to balance the demands of company reports (which focused on past activity) with meeting prospective new clients (which tied to his future quota and goals). In addition, James' perception that Bryan regularly missed meetings was skewed, undoubtedly impacted by the negativity of his mental models. The truth was that Bryan had missed three weekly meetings during the past quarter and had only done so when his clients had no other meeting times available.

The challenges were far from being one sided, however. Bryan's mental models led him to assume that James didn't value his contributions or trust his work. In Bryan's mind, no other logical explanations existed for why a sales manager would overwhelmingly micromanage a top producer.

Bryan's mental models prevented him from seeing that James was genuinely interested in his ability to consistently out-produce anyone else on the team. James wanted to understand what Bryan did differently so he could leverage the insights to improve skills and results across the board. In addition, because Bryan was so busy with his bustling book of business, he was blind to the immense pressure James received from above when reports were late, or to the disapproving glances he received when Bryan was absent from meetings.

When they both came to understand how their mental models were operating under the surface and shaping their perceptions and reactions toward one another, they were able to make positive adjustments that drastically improved their working relationship.

Mental models aren't inherently right or wrong, they just are. However, when they operate under the surface and without conscious awareness, they have the potential to negatively affect our perceptions and subsequent actions. As Peter Senge highlights in *The Fifth Discipline*, when mental models exist below the level of our awareness, they're empowered to continue unchecked and unchallenged, influencing our decision making in ways that undermine our desired goals for a different future.[1]

Uncovering these limiting belief systems is critical to growth, development, and achievement, but how do you go about catching those mental models in action before they run rampant and impact your life? This involves developing two separate yet symbiotic skills: inquiry and reflection.

With inquiry, opinions and assumptions are exchanged for questions and exploration. It's a journey to seek the questions behind the questions, with the intention of peeling back the layers until you get to the core. It's easy to form opinions and make assumptions, but it's far more difficult to challenge your assumptions, question the belief systems they evolved from, and deepen your level of inquiry.

The transformative power of questions cannot be understated. As Peter Block shares in *Community: The Structure of Belonging*, "questions open the door to the future and are more powerful than answers in that they demand engagement".[2] The moment you ask a deeper question, you've invited yourself into a process of reflection, a necessary type of engagement if the question is to be fully explored.

With reflection, deliberate time is spent in thought. Attention is focused on thinking instead of doing, and meaningful consideration is given to behaviors, thoughts, attitudes, and motivations. It involves going deeper than surface-level reactions and assumptions and requires a level of honesty and transparency about the mental models you hold in place. When consistently leveraged as a tool for growth, the benefits of reflection are far-reaching. As Dr. Geil Browning shares,

> "Reflection is a deeper form of learning that allows us to retain every aspect of any experience, be it personal or professional - why something took place, what the impact was, whether it should happen again - as opposed to just remembering *that* it happened. It's about tapping into every aspect of the experience, clarifying our thinking, and homing in on what really matters to us.

From a brain science perspective, it adds neural circuitry to your brain and expands the cerebral cortex by anchoring and deepening your experiences into learning. In layman's terms, you squeeze more benefit out of each day. Even the seemingly mundane can become great sources of ideas, provide a plethora of data to fuel personal growth, and facilitate the development of new skills."[3]

Inquiry and reflection empower you to see your mental models, challenge those that are not supportive, and shift your approach in response. This is the process both James and Bryan stepped through. We explored the perceptions they each held, questioned the assumptions these perceptions were based on, examined the belief systems that prompted these assumptions, and developed new mental models for filtering their responses and reactions through. Today, they no longer have defensive standoffs where each places the blame on the other. They both understand how their mental models play a role in creating perceptions that aren't anchored in objective truth and have learned to communicate more clearly when their individual interpretations need to be tested.

Developing a consistent cycle of inquiry and reflection takes work and commitment, but it's also key to dislodging mental models that currently stand in the way of your success. With a regular practice of inquiry and reflection, you can modify and replace existing models with those that better support your growth and propel you to achieve your future vision.

However, identifying a mental model does not immediately eradicate it. Insights are only as powerful as the intentional action leveraged to alter the habitual pattern of behavior. But as the research has shown, one of the best antidotes to unsupportive mental models is to develop a clear vision for the future (✓), connect with your values (✓), and filter your mental models accordingly.

Mental models can be intentionally designed and implemented to change the stories we tell ourselves and produce a different result. Lisa, a passionate Donor Coordinator and co-founder of a non-profit organization, learned this lesson first-hand when she attempted to shift her mental model surrounding challenge #4, Welcoming Distractions. Lisa had noticed that over the last several months she had allowed increasingly more distractions to disrupt her days. The pattern of behavior had become so evident that her business partner felt it necessary to gently address it with her.

As Lisa inquired more deeply into the pattern of behavior that had developed, she asked herself:

- Why do I let so many distractions in?
- Why am I not firmer with my boundaries?
- What would happen if I placed higher value on how I spend my time?
- If I limited distractions, what could I achieve with the extra time gained in a day, week, or month?

As Lisa explored each question, she reflected on the interlacing insights that arose, realizing that "welcoming distractions" had become a defense strategy for her. It armed her with a built-in excuse for why she wasn't making progress toward their larger goals - after all, other people were always interrupting her progress therefore *they* were to blame.

When she peeled back the layers even further, her reflections revealed that this lack of progress prevented her from experiencing any failure associated with trying but not succeeding. While she had never voiced it, she was afraid that the goals and vision of their venture had outgrown her skill set. She was standing at the outer edge of her comfort zone and "welcoming distractions" protected her from having to deal with her fear.

This eye-opening insight forced her to acknowledge that the safety embedded in her defense-based approach was actually limiting her growth while constraining the overall success of the organization. It was in the depths of this awareness that her ultimate a-ha arose. She was acting from a fixed mindset that viewed stumbles as failures instead of opportunities for learning and growth.

Lisa was initially baffled by this discovery - especially given that she held 'learning' as one of her core values. But as she refocused on her vision for the future, which largely revolved around securing funding for their non-profit youth education program, she realized she had to restructure her mental model surrounding distractions.

Now, instead of viewing them as fun opportunities to connect and catch up with others, she crafted a visual image that likened distractions to the big brake lever that slows down a train. Each time the brake is pulled, it slowed down her journey and lengthened the amount of time it would take to pull into the final station. This new mental model led to a massive shift in how she viewed and treated her time. She was now far more protective of it knowing the value it held to improve the lives of others through the initiatives of the non-profit.

This is not to say Lisa's life became 100% distraction free, but the image associated with the new mental model helped her prioritize how her time was spent during working hours. Rather than allowing distractions to dictate the flow of her day, Lisa set specific hours for when distractions were welcomed or allowed. Her new routine has her proactively encouraging friends and colleagues to reach out between 11:30 am and 1 pm, or better yet, to join her for lunch. She also draws firm boundaries around her morning and afternoon work blocks so that distractions no longer derail her efforts. Doing so has allowed her to speed up her train, while also leaving additional learning time to further cultivate her growth mindset.

Not everyone will suffer from all seven challenges, but it's important to take note of which ones affect you and how they actively shape your decision making. You do get a choice - either your mental models can unconsciously influence you, or you can deliberately choose to influence them. Which will you choose?

On the Path to Becoming

When we gain an understanding of the mental models that shape us and contrast them against our vision for the future, it empowers us to explore who we need to become in order to make that future a reality. The person you are today is not the same person you were five years ago, and who you will be five years from now, when living fully into your vision, is not who you are today. The question becomes, what do you have to do today to become your future self?

Discovering the answer requires a process of inquiry and reflection that includes connecting with your vision and values at a deeper level, acknowledging growth areas that need to be addressed, and taking actions that are in alignment with your future self. In the depths of inquiry and reflection lies the path that empowers you to bridge the gap between who you are and who you're becoming.

⇒ **Exercise #1**: To embark on a deliberate journey of inquiry and reflection - one that is intentionally designed to put you on the path to who you're becoming - begin by re-reading both your vivid vision and the personal definitions you constructed surrounding your values. Then, answer the following questions (which are inquiry and reflection in action) to help you identify the gaps between your current and future selves. Space for doing so has been provided beginning on page 23 of your workbook.

1. Are there any values reflected in your vision and held by your future self that you don't actively hold today? List these values and create a personal definition for each one.

2. Are there certain values you need to elevate and live into more fully? List the values and write out why they need to be a bigger priority in your life.

3. What actions can you take to bring these values to the forefront of your life? Be specific and detailed.

4. What skills do you need to develop in order to support your vision? An example might include learning to use LinkedIn so you can network with others. List the skills, note why they're important, and detail how they'll support your journey.

5. What activities does your future self need you to engage in today? An example might include taking a course that teaches you how to best use LinkedIn. List each activity and note how it positively serves your future self.

6. Which of your mental models (belief systems) serve you well? Be specific and include how these belief systems support your future self.

7. Which of your mental models do you need to refine or replace? Be specific and detailed, outlining how they will hold you back if they remain in place.

8. Is your time currently spent in ways that support the development of your future vision? Outline a typical day and evaluate if your future self needs you to reallocate how your time is spent. Specifically, detail anything you'll do differently going forward.

9. Are you surrounding yourself with the type of people that the future you needs? Take inventory of your circle of influence, including friends, family, colleagues, and anyone whom you regularly interact with. List the person's name, the qualities they bring to the

relationship, and whether or not your future self would choose to interact with them.

10. Are there any unsupportive relationships that you need to release? Looking at your relationship inventory above, determine if you need to make any changes and outline how you will go about doing so.

11. Do your digital habits support your future self? List the sites, channels, apps, and services you regularly engage with. Does the content and messaging support who you're becoming or does your future self need you to make some adjustments?

12. Are the materials you read and absorb contributing to who you're becoming? List the types of books, magazines and articles you regularly read and evaluate if they're contributing to your future vision. If not, detail any changes you'll make.

Once you've answered the above questions and reflected on the insights that surfaced for you, ask yourself: *What changes are required to put yourself on the path toward who you're becoming?* Identify your top three priorities for taking action and living into your future self now.

Inquiry and reflection are invaluable tools that can dissolve the boundaries of limitation. When we intentionally use these tools to reflect more deeply on the alignment between our current circumstances, our visions and values, and who we need to be in order to live fully into these, it sparks intrinsic motivation, driving us to become our best future selves. Inquiry and reflection prime our psychological pump, strengthening who we are as well as who we are becoming, and putting us on a meaningful path toward self-actualization.

Before moving into part two, compare your answers from this chapter's exercise with your vision statement. Does your vision need to be revised or updated in any way? If so, take the time to make those adjustments before moving on. Remember, the strength of this book and program lies not with the words that line the pages but rather, in the thoughts, reflections, inquiries, and insights that surface from you throughout the process.

part two

Discovering Strengths and Adapting Behaviors

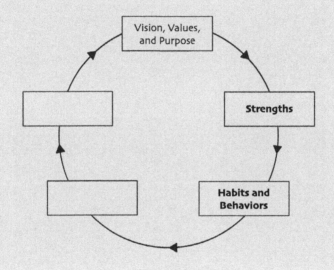

chapter five

Discovering Your Strengths

"The path to great leadership starts with a deep understanding of the strengths you bring to the table."

- Tom Rath

Anne's Story

"Frankly, we believe you get too involved with your team. If you want to move up in this company, you need to learn to take the bull by the horns and lead more forcefully. Don't spend so much time working side-by-side with your direct reports. Lead - don't join. Give your team clear instructions and set concrete expectations, but don't do their jobs with them. And if they get something wrong or don't meet expectations, hold them accountable. Senior management consistently notes that you're *too* nice and it's affecting your promotion opportunities."

This is the feedback Anne, a sales manager for a large, multinational organization, received during her annual review. The words hit her like a ton of bricks, forcing her to question the aspirations she held for eventually growing into an executive leadership position. She left the meeting feeling confused and perplexed, especially since her team was in the top 5% of producers company-wide and she was highly regarded by employees and clients alike. She had a reputation for developing talent, was known to genuinely care about her teammates, and regularly celebrated the accomplishments of those around her. Rarely did positions open up on her team, but when they did, it was not uncommon for a long list of internal employees to eagerly apply.

On most days, Anne went home feeling proud of the leader she was. But on the day she contacted me, she was feeling quite discouraged by the feedback she'd received. Her leadership style had an undeniably positive influence on her team, so why wasn't it valued more highly by those above her? The comments were beginning to erode her confidence and she started questioning herself, her career, and her worth.

As we progressed through the initial phases of our coaching relationship, it was important that she discover, connect, and reflect on the unique combination of character strengths that she brought to the equation. On this basis, she took a strengths assessment which revealed that her signature strengths (a term you'll learn more about shortly) were Kindness, Teamwork, Love of Learning, Social Intelligence, and Perspective, in that order. This impactful blend of strengths spoke directly to the high regard others held for her as a leader, yet she was initially dismissive of their immense value. Her gaze immediately focused on the fact that "Leadership" itself had turned out to be a middle strength and not a top one - a result she was judging herself harshly for.

Unfortunately, Anne's unfavorable reaction follows a typical pattern. Human nature often leads us to actively seek out perceived weaknesses and focus on those first, but as the research has shown, this approach anchors us in the NEA, triggers the sympathetic nervous system, and limits growth and development.[1] Knowing this, the first step was to shift Anne's attention back to her signature strengths and identify examples of how these strengths positively shaped her work life on a daily basis.

Her Kindness was consistently woven throughout the interpersonal approach she took in supporting her team and continually fostering their personal and professional growth. She frequently gifted books, tools, and other resources that benefitted their individual journeys - a gesture that made each employee feel truly seen. Evidence of her Teamwork was continuously on display in the approach she took in working *with* her group instead of above them, demonstrating the value she placed on succeeding together. Her Love of Learning was showcased in the view she held of herself as a mentor and coach who was there to learn as much as possible and, in turn, share the knowledge with her team. Her Social Intelligence empowered her to understand and empathize with the feelings and experiences of others, supportively adapting to different situations and personalities in the process. And lastly, her Perspective repeatedly surfaced when her reps would lose a sale and she would focus on the positives first, helping them to identify what they did well in the process before looking for the lessons embedded in the loss.

The exploration of her strengths in action began to dramatically shift how she viewed herself and her contributions as a leader. As her recollections grew in detail, her countenance changed dramatically, and her PEA responded in kind. Suddenly, the feedback from her review didn't feel quite so heavy or demoralizing. The dark, stormy cloud that had dampened her outlook had given way to a bright sunshiny sky and she was now keenly aware of the value of her strengths, proud of the positive ways they supported her team, and eager to continually embrace them with her own unique style.

We'll return to Anne's story later in this chapter, but first let's explore exactly what character strengths are, the science behind them, and the role they play in helping us to step into our future vision and become our best selves.

The History of Character Strengths

Over the course of a 3-year project, Chris Peterson and Martin Seligman led 55 notable and globally dispersed scientists, researchers, and scholars on an exhaustive exploration into the science of human flourishing. Their initial goal was to bring balance to the field of psychology, which, up until that point, had primarily focused on disorders, diseases, and maladaptive behaviors. But knowing humans are comprised of far more than just their challenges and weaknesses, Peterson and Seligman began a journey to uncover and identify the positive traits that are foundational to well-being. They sought to move beyond the negative association of flaws and identify the positive traits that paved the path to flourishing.

Their deep dive began with an extensive historical review on the topics of character, virtue, and human goodness, analyzing more than 2,500 years' worth of research, insights, and wisdom drawn from the teachings of psychology, philosophy, virtue ethics, moral education, and theology.[2] This allowed them to identify a common language for defining what is best in humans, and then to extrapolate a classification of six virtues (wisdom, courage, humanity, justice, temperance, and transcendence), which were found to be universally applicable, transcending the boundaries of religion, culture, socioeconomic status, belief systems, and nation of origin. These are the virtues that, across time and space, have consistently been proven to contribute to a meaningful life.

With the classification of virtues established, ten empirically tested criteria for identifying and determining character strengths were constructed, empowering the research team to identify 24 universal strengths which are now known as the VIA Character Strengths.

When practiced and developed, these strengths become the psychological ingredients that support a person living into the virtues.[3] As noted by Neal H. Mayerson, PhD, it was "the most comprehensive and robust effort ever to understand what's best about human beings and how we build full and flourishing lives for ourselves and others".[4]

The 24 character strengths, and the respective virtue categories they support, are:

- Virtue of Wisdom: Creativity, Curiosity, Judgment, Love of Learning, Perspective

- Virtue of Courage: Bravery, Perseverance, Honesty, Zest

- Virtue of Humanity: Love, Kindness, Social Intelligence

- Virtue of Justice: Teamwork, Fairness, Leadership

- Virtue of Temperance: Forgiveness, Humility, Prudence, Self-Regulation

- Virtue of Transcendence: Appreciation of Beauty and Excellence, Gratitude, Hope, Humor, Spirituality

As humans, we have a variety of strengths we use within a given day. There are **talents**, which are strengths we're naturally and inherently good at; **skills**, which are strengths we've intentionally cultivated and developed; **interests**, which surface as areas of passion and intrigue; and **values**, which shape our thoughts and emotions. Character strengths, however, can be viewed as "values in action" (VIA) that cut across the other strength domains and produce the actions and behaviors that shape *who* we are, not just *what* we do.

A person can have an incredible talent for playing the piano, but without leveraging the character strengths of *perseverance* and *self-regulation*, may never develop into a world-class player. Someone may possess a natural knack for coding, but without *self-regulation* and a *love of learning*, they may fall short of acquiring the education and experience necessary to pursue a career in coding. A person who has an interest in social justice but lacks the *curiosity* to explore it further or the *zest* to approach it with energy and excitement may find their interest quickly wanes.

Character strengths act as the yellow brick road that helps guide us toward our vision, dreams, and goals. When understood and intentionally practiced, they become a conduit that brings our vision and values into alignment with the behaviors and habits of our future self. They supercharge who we are and who we are becoming. To understand how and why this is so, let's take a closer look at some of the research findings.

The Science of Character Strengths

While there is no one-size-fits-all approach to human flourishing, there is an empirically supported theory that underpins what enables it: the PERMA theory of well-being. (If this sounds familiar, it's because you took the PERMA assessment at the beginning of this program.) PERMA - **P**ositive Emotion, **E**ngagement, **R**elationships, **M**eaning, and **A**ccomplishment - are the building blocks of happiness and well-being. While the contributing value of each component varies according to the person, understanding the basis of these foundational blocks, and how character strengths encourage and support their development, enables people to live more meaningful and fulfilling lives.

Positive Emotion: Positive feelings such as joy, love, hope, gratitude, and compassion, that elicit positive emotional thoughts and contribute to supportive, favorable emotions. While this is often one of the more obvious aspects of happiness and well-being, what's frequently overlooked are the deliberate, action-oriented ways that we can influence our positive emotions through the intentional use of our character strengths. It's important to acknowledge that everyone has a different positive emotion baseline which is influenced by our genetic disposition, but even those who find it more difficult to experience positive emotions regularly can impact their equation with intentional effort. As the research has shown, increasing the time spent in a positive emotional state contributes to an increase in physical, intellectual, social, and psychological resources[5] while simultaneously undoing the effects of negative emotions[6] and building resilience.[7]

Character Strengths that contribute to, and correlate most with, **Positive Emotion** *include:* Humor, Zest, Hope, Curiosity, Social Intelligence, Bravery, and Love[8,16]

Engagement: Being fully engaged in an activity to the point where one loses track of time and enters a state of all-consuming flow. As Mihaly Csikszentmihalyi, renowned researcher on the subject of flow has documented, flow arises at the boundary between boredom and anxiety, where skills, strengths, and effort combine to meet a challenging task.[9] When one is fully engaged and engrossed in the task at hand, the activity becomes its own reward. Self-awareness disappears as one becomes fully enmeshed in their experience, creating a space where time appears to stand still.[10] Flow can be experienced through a variety of activities, such as having a great conversation with a dear friend, reading a captivating book, spending time on a favorite hobby, or going for a hike in nature, just to name a few.

Character Strengths that contribute to, and correlate most with, **Engagement** *include:* Persistence, Hope, Creativity, Curiosity, Humor, Love of Learning, Perseverance, Zest, Leadership, and Self-Regulation[11,17]

Relationships: Developing and engaging in supportive, social connections with others. Research has shown that individuals with close social relationships have higher levels of well-being and hold increased levels of hope and optimism toward a desirable future.[12] Positive relationships have repeatedly been shown to be a fundamental component of well-being, acting as an antidote to life's struggles and creating a reliable method of improving one's mood.[13] Experiences are often amplified when shared, such as when you tell a friend about a funny incident and the two of you laugh together, a process that further contributes to well-being and relationship building.[14]

Character Strengths that contribute to, and correlate most with, **Relationships** *include*: Love, Kindness, Teamwork, Gratitude, and Forgiveness[15,18]

Meaning: A sense of purpose that is bigger than one's self and incorporates feelings of belonging.[19] Meaning is derived from serving others but can be achieved in a myriad of ways. As examples, some may find meaning through the profession they chose and the contribution it makes to their field, others may experience it through their support of a social justice cause (such as climate change or inequality), and some may choose to write books that address a certain need or serve a specific population. The list is endless, and the approaches are both personal and individualized, but the common denominator revolves around a focus that is larger than one's self.

Character Strengths that contribute to, and correlate most with, **Meaning** *include*: Curiosity, Hope, Zest, Perspective, Social Intelligence, Appreciation of Beauty and Excellence, Gratitude, and Spirituality[20,21]

Accomplishment: Achieving a goal or mastering an area of interest for its own sake and not exclusively as a means to an end.[22] Efforts devoted toward crafting a vision and achieving the respective goals brings about a burgeoning sense of accomplishment that sparks motivation and drives self-efficacy. Interestingly, it's commonly difficult to acknowledge gains as they unfold because accomplishment is often retrospective; it comes when we achieve a particular milestone and can look back on the achievement with pride and joy.[23]

Character Strengths that contribute to, and correlate most with, **Accomplishment** *include*: Hope, Persistence, Zest, Curiosity, Bravery, Perspective, Love, Love of Learning, Leadership, Social Intelligence, and Self-Regulation[24, 25]

Character strengths are "basic building blocks of a flourishing life", acting as "pathways to well-being".[26] As we'll explore further in the next section, when character strengths are used intentionally and consistently, happiness and well-being increase, empowering us to flourish and thrive as we travel the path towards our goals and dreams.

Character Strengths in Action

Among the many contributions that Peterson and Seligman's exploration into human flourishing brought about was the creation of the VIA Character Strengths Assessment, an empirically supported psychometric measurement of individual character strengths, and the VIA Institute on Character, which provides resources, tools, and education for practitioners looking to take the application of character strengths to the next level. At the end of this chapter, I'll provide a link for you to take the VIA Character Strengths Assessment, but there are a few important aspects to understand before you do.

While the assessment provides an ordered list of how one ranks for all 24 strengths, none are "weaknesses", not even the last one on the list. Each of us possess and use all 24 strengths at different times, though some may come more naturally while others may be used less frequently or only on a situational basis. As an example, someone may find bravery to be a lower strength, yet countless examples exist in their lives when they mustered up the courage and bravery to tackle something difficult. In this case, bravery is a "phasic strength", meaning that the individual doesn't lead with this strength, but strategically uses it when a situation calls for it.

The three categories individual strengths fall into are signature, middle, and lower strengths.

Signature Strengths: Those strengths which are most central and core to who we are. These are the go-to strengths that are leveraged most often because they come easily and naturally. Signature strengths frequently serve as an energizing and rejuvenating source when put to use and are often the strengths at play when we find ourselves in a state of flow. To validate the importance of signature strengths, look at your top five strengths and imagine what life would be like if one of your key strengths was suddenly taken away. Would it change or alter who you are at your core?

Middle Strengths: Sometimes referred to as "supportive strengths", middle strengths support and/or enhance our signature strengths. They're like the salt that gets added to a recipe; they don't change the core flavor profile but when used in the right proportions, significantly enhance it.

Lower Strengths: These strengths are generally used less frequently than signature and middle strengths, largely because they do not come as naturally or easily. Sometimes they are underdeveloped or underused compared to other strengths in our profile, and sometimes they are phasic strengths which are only used situationally. However, they are not weaknesses and can be bolstered, if one chooses to do so.

It's important to note that character traits are not fixed; they can be developed and strengthened with intentional effort. If a person determines that their future self needs a certain strength to be enhanced, deliberate effort toward developing that strength will produce positive results. (You can explore strength-specific exercises in the appendix, after you complete the assessment.) In addition, while the research shows that all 24 character strengths contribute positively to well-being and happiness in varying degrees, the highest overall correlations across the PERMA dimensions occurred with Hope, Zest, Curiosity, Love of Learning, and Creativity.[27]

It can be helpful to view character strengths like muscles. The more you actively practice and use them, the more they grow and serve you. But like all muscles, it's equally important to note that they can be over or underused. Each strength exists on a continuum where optimum use is created from a balanced approach but sliding too far toward either end diminishes its use and value.

As an example, someone with a balanced approach to bravery will find they are able to optimally utilize this strength when facing fears and confronting adversity. However, an overuse may result in an unhealthy and potentially dangerous foolhardiness, while someone who underuses it may approach challenges with an unsupportive cowardice. The continuum of optimal use for each individual character strength is provided in the appendix.

Lastly, sometimes I'm asked why a particular character trait isn't reflected in the VIA Character Assessment. As an example, a client recently inquired about "patience", sharing that she felt strongly this was one of her top strengths. And it was - just not in the way she expected. Patience is an example of a "compound strength" that is drawn from a combination of strengths. In this case, patience emerges from the combination of Perseverance, Self-Regulation, and Judgment. Two of those were among her signature strengths while the third was a high middle strength. With a deeper understanding of how strengths stand alone and combine to make her who she is, she felt more empowered to create the results her future self was seeking.

As an aside... **Strengths-spotting is a powerful tool for developing the leader within.** Just as the name describes, strengths-spotting is the deliberate process of actively looking for the use of strengths in yourself and others. Doing so inherently shifts the natural focus away from what's wrong within a given situation and puts the emphasis on what's right.

This proven method for developing your own strengths while simultaneously bolstering those of others puts the emphasis on the positive and moves away from the deficit-minded approach that far too often plagues relational interactions and perceptions. Strengths-spotting empowers us to better understand the people we work with, gain new insights into our family and friends, and see movies and TV shows through a new lens. When we learn to focus on the strengths each individual brings to the table, we naturally begin to deepen our empathy, a trait and skill that positively enhances the leadership equation and allows us to connect more deeply with others.[28,29]

The appendix includes a deeper dive on each individual strength, providing examples of each strength in action, an understanding of under, over, and optimal use, suggested actions for building each strength, and a film recommendation that paints a wonderful picture of each strength in practice. Armed with these insights, you can implement the three variations of strengths-spotting below.

- Choose a strength as your theme for the day, then consciously be on the lookout for any and all examples that arise. You may see evidence of it in yourself, it may surface in the friends, family, and colleagues who surround you, you may witness it in the interactions between complete strangers as you run errands, or you may see it on display in your favorite TV show. As you see the selected strength surface, try to identify as many unique expressions of it as possible, bringing to awareness the myriad of ways that strengths can shape our daily activities and interactions.

- When a relationship, be it personal or professional, is experiencing discord, devote a day (at a minimum) to looking for the various strengths that the other person repeatedly brings to the equation. As an example, if you find yourself consistently annoyed with a co-worker who asks so many questions that they slow down progress, you may come to realize that their questions are actually fueled by a strong sense of curiosity which positively serves the work environment, occasionally uncovering challenges that others didn't consider. Reframing our perspectives to focus on the strengths in others can go a long way toward enhancing our relationships.

- Think back to a recent time when you were running on all cylinders and performing at your best. Picture as many details as possible, including what you were actively doing, who else was involved, any aspects that naturally flowed, and the final outcome produced in the process. As you replay the scenario in your mind, ask yourself which strengths were most prevalent during the event. Were your signature strengths in the driver's seat? Did you find a middle or lesser strength rose to the occasion? What made the event so memorable from a strengths-based perspective?

If you'd like to download a one-page pdf that lists all 24 strengths, categorizes them according to the virtue they support, and gives you an easy reference point for strengths-spotting, visit:
http://lwm.link/24strengths.

Every individual is a unique combination of their strengths. When focus is shifted away from perceived weaknesses and emphasis is placed on personal strengths, it has lasting, positive effects on health, well-being, happiness, and life satisfaction.[30] Anne experienced this transformation first-hand. After taking the assessment and exploring examples of her strengths in action, she was able to see how Leadership, as a middle strength, was supporting her signature strengths of Kindness, Teamwork, Love of Learning, Social Intelligence, and Perspective.

Anne also realized that her brand of leadership, as defined, supported, and enhanced by her signature strengths, fit with the future vision she held for her career and life. Moving up the corporate ladder was important to her, but her reason for wanting to do so was clarified when she filtered her vision and values through her signature strengths.

Anne realized that her motivation to become an executive was driven by her desire to help individuals grow and develop, both personally and professionally. She believed that organizations who prioritized mentoring and development as part of their workplace culture would flourish and thrive, and further, that stronger, happier, more productive employees would evolve in the process.

For years she had experienced this with her own small team, but she now desired the opportunity to positively impact a much larger group. This forced her to introspect on how the culture within her current workplace was at odds with her future vision, a realization that led to her updating her resumé. As Stephen Covey once said, "if the ladder is not leaning against the right wall, every step we take just gets us to the wrong place faster". She knew her ladder was against the wrong wall and began taking steps to move it. Within six months, she had secured a new opportunity as a District Sales Director overseeing a sales force of 2,500 professionals. She continues to thrive in this challenging yet rewarding role where her signature strengths, vision, and values intersect in greatness.

Are you ready to amplify your vision and values with the power of your strengths? Visit **http://lwm.link/strengths** to take the VIA Character Strengths assessment, then record your strengths on page 26 of your workbook. Once you've completed the assessment and captured the results, visit the appendix to learn more about your individual strengths and how they can be intentionally leveraged to fuel your success and improve your results.

chapter six

Powering Success with Supportive Habits

"We are what we repeatedly do. Excellence, then, is not an act but a habit."

- Aristotle

Sheryl's Story

Sheryl was the type of middle manager that every executive leader looked for and every hourly employee appreciated. She was dedicated to her job and her team and took great pride in consistently hitting her department's targets and goals. She was the go-to person for getting things done and was widely revered throughout the organization.

However, she'd been in the same role for nearly three years and was frustrated by having been passed over for two different promotions. She loved the company, was aligned with the culture and values, and wanted to grow with the organization, but was unsure if the opportunity to do so would ever present itself. Despite her frustrations, she continued to show up and shine every day, bringing her best self to the office and consistently excelling in her role.

As happenstance would have it, she was grabbing lunch one Saturday at a local deli when she bumped into Chuck, an Executive Vice President from her company. Chuck invited her to join him at his table and the two began chatting. Small talk at first, but eventually the conversation evolved to include the exciting company growth that was currently taking place. Sheryl shared how much she enjoyed working there and voiced the pride she took in being part of the workplace family, but Chuck intuitively sensed a shift in her demeanor and a bit of hesitation in her voice.

Responding to her cues, Chuck asked her where she saw herself in five years. Much to her own surprise, the words leapt from her lips before she could stop them. "I really want to move into a position where I can have a larger impact on the company. I love my job, but I feel limited in my role and I want to make a bigger difference - that's why I was so intrigued by the area director position."

Chuck was surprised to hear her response, largely because he wasn't aware that Sheryl had been interested in the area director position or that she had higher aspirations. From his perspective, she seemed comfortable and confident with the role she was in, almost to a fault. To his knowledge, she had never approached the executive leadership team regarding a desire to increase her responsibilities, nor had he witnessed her displaying a personal interest in her corporate growth and development. Instead, what he saw was a wonderful, consistent manager who was a highly valued asset to those around her but who never seemed to stretch herself beyond her comfort zone.

Chuck gently shared his perspectives with Sheryl, which were initially difficult for her to hear, but after they parted ways, she realized how truly insightful and important the feedback was. For the first time, she was able to see herself through the eyes of those above her and realized that her comfortability in her role had actually created a pattern of passivity that was holding her back. True, she enthusiastically approached her work on a daily basis, but always within the safe bounds of her comfort zone.

Sheryl had developed a set of habits and behaviors that were seemingly positive on the surface but were equally limiting to her potential. Coming face to face with this reality, she was hit with the fundamental truth that if you do what you've always done, you'll get what you've always got. In order to change your life, you must change your habits.

How Habits Can Help or Hinder

In chapters two through four, considerable effort and energy was invested in connecting with your values and clearly articulating your vision. You brought your vivid vision to life, both in words and in your mind's eye, while ensuring it complemented your core values. In chapter five, you discovered your unique combination of strengths and learned how they could be leveraged as a superpower to spur greater achievement. Your hard work to this point sets the stage for a different future, but sadly, the potential exists for these efforts to fall flat without a concrete understanding of the habits that underpin your everyday efforts.

Just as yesterday's habits and behaviors shape today's realities, all your tomorrows will be based on your habits of today. Yet, a striking number of people are unaware of the engrained habits that support or diminish their activities and achievements. Accordingly, it's critical to understand exactly how habits work and what steps can be taken to alter, adopt, or release them in support of your future self. For this reason, the next step in the process involves peeling back the layers of habit, uncovering those that are both supporting and hindering your progress, and learning how to adapt your behaviors to intentionally support the pursuit of your goals.

While it's commonly understood that habits are patterns of behavior that become second nature over time, Charles Duhigg points out an important distinction in *The Power of Habit*. As Duhigg shares, a habit is initially a behavior made by *choice* which becomes automatic with consistent practice over time.[1] The beauty of his explanation is that it lays the groundwork for a deeper understanding of how unhelpful habits can be released or altered, and how supportive, new habits can be implemented. As he outlines, habits occur in three-part loops which begin with an external cue that triggers the habit loop, a subsequent routine made up of consistent behaviors performed in response to the cue, and a reward that reinforces the habitual repetition of the routine.[2] Cue. Routine. Reward.

Habit loops themselves aren't positive or negative - they just are. Whether or not they support growth and development, however, is a different story. As an example, a client of mine struggled to stay focused and on-task with everyday work assignments, creating a stressful environment that left him perpetually chasing his tail.

When we initially began working together, he was convinced the company was at fault, giving him more tasks than 8-hours a day would allow for. However, it quickly became evident that his habits were the real culprit of his strife. Each time his email notification would pop up (cue), he would immediately stop what he was doing to check the email (routine). Responding right away filled him with a sense of pride (reward), even though his responses often relayed that he was still working on the issue at hand and would get back to the sender soon. Incoming phone calls were handled the same way, consistently chipping blocks of time away from his day.

When he understood that this habit loop was hurting his productivity rather than helping it, he was able to amend his approach. He turned off his email notifications and allocated specific times during the day when he would check and respond to email. In addition, he started using an alarm on his phone (cue) to indicate when he would begin a focused block of work to complete tasks without disruption (routine). The rewards were two-fold.

Firstly, he felt a much deeper sense of accomplishment because he was now able to complete his daily tasks in a timely fashion, which motivated him to continue implementing this new habit loop (reward 1). Secondly, others in the organization acknowledged his progress and commented on his improvements, which further reinforced his new behavior while filling him with the same sense of pride that had been anchored in the original habit loop (reward 2). To Duhigg's point, my client's new work habit was initially a behavior made by choice which became automatic with consistent practice over time.

Habits drive actions and behaviors. Intentionally align your habits with your vision, values, and future self and those habits become supercharged, harnessing the potential to power your success. Allow your habits to unconsciously set their own agenda, and you're forced to exert self-control as you attempt to overcome negative behavior patterns.

As research published in the *Journal of Personality and Social Psychology* highlighted, beneficial habits that are in support of one's goals decrease the need for and use of self-control, a capacity that is easily compromised in the face of stress or tiredness.[3] In other words, trying to rely strictly on self-control as a method for avoiding behaviors that detract from goal achievement may be a fool's errand due to the significant effort that self-control requires. This becomes quickly evident when one holds certain health and fitness goals, but then gives into their junk food craving with little to no fight after an overly stressful day.

The role of everyday stressors is an important point of consideration. As the research has shown, stressors decrease our ability to make wise, advantageous choices, diminishing our decision-making capacity in the process.[4] Put another way, stress causes us to make poor decisions we might not otherwise make. However, when we intentionally create habits that support our growth and development, we can eliminate some elements of decision-making from our equation by constructing systems that put certain behaviors on autopilot.

As a personal example, donuts used to be my kryptonite, especially when they travelled that amazing journey under the waterfall of glorious glaze and came straight off the Krispy Kreme conveyor belt. However, eating these sinfully delicious morsels of mouthwatering goodness didn't support my health and wellness goals. In addition, the immediate and negative impacts caused by the direct injection of sugar, including a depletion in energy levels and a decrease in mental clarity, often prevented me from doing my best work for the remainder of the day. I knew I needed a better way to tackle this challenge, and it had to be one that didn't rely on self-control.

My solution began with a new habit of keeping a donut-flavored protein bar in my workbag at all times – a ONE bar, for those who also need a healthy donut alternative. When I'm at a meeting or in an environment where donuts are trying to tempt and tease me with their tantalizing allure, I allow my supportive habit loop to kick in. The smell of fresh donuts (cue) leads me to reach for my protein bar (routine) which then fills me with a sense of pride and control because I am living a deliberate life in alignment with my health and fitness goals (reward).

Ensuring habits are in alignment with one's values, vision, and goals is a conscious, purposeful choice. It doesn't happen by accident or default - it only happens when one chooses to start living life by design.

4-Steps to Habit Identification: Uncover, Evaluate, Choose, Apply

A deep dive into the science of habits, which included reviewing myriad research studies, reading dozens of books, watching countless interviews, and studying the patterns of successful habit formation, led me to a powerful insight. Buried in the cross-pollination of all this research were four distinct steps to habit identification: Uncover, Evaluate, Choose, Apply.

From a big picture perspective, one cannot incorporate positive, future-oriented habits unless and until they *uncover* the current habits that shape their daily experiences. Once awareness is applied and habits are uncovered, the next step is to *evaluate* if the habits are supporting one's goals and desires or detracting from them. Armed with these insights, the next step is to *choose* what adjustments, if any, need to be made. And the final step is to *apply* the adjustments and alter the behavior.

While the above steps create a simple framework to follow, simple isn't always easy. Habit identification is a process that requires attention and effort but pays large dividends in return. It's also important to note that the process of habit identification is not a quick, one-and-done exercise. It's a practice, by definition, and as such requires repetitive application to produce meaningful insights that lead to measurable results. The discoveries made by revisiting this process repeatedly over time allows one to perpetually uncover, evaluate, choose, and apply supportive habits that promote ongoing success.

However, a quick word of caution must be issued before we proceed. The quickest road to frustration is to try to change all your unsupportive habits at once. This is a recipe for disaster that has repeatedly proven to create a whirlwind of overwhelm that causes people to abandon their initiatives nearly as quickly as they adopt them. The key to avoiding this pitfall is to hone one or two habits at a time, and once they're operating on autopilot, add in one or two more. With that important point established, let's explore the 4-steps to Habit Identification.

Uncover

Uncovering your current habits requires self-awareness and personal reflection to identify the unconscious behaviors that drive your daily actions and create your end results. One of the best ways to practice this type of self-awareness is by using your Curiosity character strength (see appendix) to ask questions, then explore the answers that surface as a result. In addition, walking through your day chronologically can help target your curiosity as you navigate the habit identification discovery path.

⇒ **Exercise #1a: Uncover.** Reflect on the following questions, which are also included on page 27 of your downloadable workbook, to help you get jump-started with the process:

- What's the first thing you do when you wake up in the morning? Do you have purposeful habits that set the tone for a positive day? Do you begin the day on autopilot, mindlessly going through the same actions today as yesterday? Do you wake up in a reactionary mode, beginning with a reaction to the alarm clock and continuing from there? Detail how you start the day and the impacts your morning routine has on your mood.

- Do you take actions in the morning that positively contribute to your physical health? How about your mental and emotional health? And what about your spiritual well-being? Does your morning routine serve to positively kick off your day?

- How early in your day do you check email or social media notifications? After your digital check-in, do you find yourself feeling rushed to dig into the day and respond? Do you see any evidence of digital habits putting you in a reactionary mode as opposed to you taking control and proactively setting your own priorities?

- How do you fuel your body in the morning? Do you eat a nourishing breakfast? Do you drink caffeine, and if so, is this habit within healthy boundaries or does it teeter towards excessiveness?

- Do you typically arrive early, on time, or late for daily obligations, such as going to work, participating in meetings, or heading to appointments? How do your patterns of timeliness benefit or harm your mental game? Do you arrive calm and ready, or hurried and rushed?

- When you sit down to start your workday, are you clear on the initiatives you'll tackle first? Do you have defined goals and strategic priorities that set the tone for your day? Do you allow others to dictate

the cadence of your day by reactively giving priority to incoming emails and voicemails?
- Do you deliberately design tomorrow's successes by proactively planning for them today?

While this list of questions is nowhere close to exhaustive, putting yourself in the mindset of walking through each step of your day can be quite revealing. Devon, a sales manager for a software solutions firm, found himself rather surprised by what surfaced for him during this process. He had long been frustrated by consistently feeling rushed and hurried from morning to night. His mornings were slowed down by an energetic dog that needed walking but refused to stay focused on the task at hand, and by his enthusiastic kids, whose morning routine more closely resembled a scene from Lord of the Flies.

The professional order he craved at the office was equally elusive. He regularly found himself racing into the building, just barely arriving on time for his daily team kick-off call, before rushing back out to his first client meeting of the day. And so went his day, with a frenetic pace that left little space for proactivity and put him in a constant state of reacting to everything around him.

When we first began exploring this challenge, Devon attributed his frustrations to external factors and forces that were out of his control. The kids, the dog, the meeting schedule - what choice did he have besides running as fast as possible to stay caught up on the treadmill of life? He was owning his role as a dedicated family man and doing what he felt had to do, both personally and professionally.

But was he really? What Devon would soon discover was that this pattern was the result of his personal habits - habits that were absolutely within his control to change.

As we began exploring the questions above, several important revelations surfaced for Devon. For starters, the first thing he did each morning was hit the snooze button... twice... to eke out every last ounce of sleep. When his feet finally hit the floor, he was instantly rushed, hurrying through his shower and morning routine, knowing he had to walk the dog and feed the kids before his wife, a fitness instructor at the local gym, returned home from teaching her morning class. When she walked in the door, she would take over parenting duties, getting the kids dressed and off to school, while Devon hurried out the door to get to work.

He would race to the office to hold the morning meeting, followed by a quick glance at his calendar to see the appointments and calls that would fill his day. Given his role as the sales manager, he made his calendar open and available for his team to book him on sales calls, but he had no process for ensuring there was space between these appointments. As a result, his entire day was spent rushing between meetings and calls, with little to no time to return phone calls or respond to emails.

Once Devon began walking through each aspect of his day, it didn't take long for him to *uncover* the habits that were contributing to his rushed and hurried day. With a few key habits uncovered, we moved to the evaluation phase.

Evaluate

When reflection and introspection are employed to uncover habits, insights arise that empower the nature of those habits to be evaluated through a fresh lens. Suddenly, valuable distance arises between you and the habit, allowing for a better understanding of the role it plays in your life and how it impacts or affects other habits. Frequently, this introspection process leads to the awareness that habit chains resembling a line of dominoes exist in our lives; trigger the first one and a series of others follows on its heels. Sometimes, the chain is beneficial and supportive, enhancing our mental game and setting our day up for success. But other times, the first habit is responsible for a reactionary chain that undermines our ultimate progress.

How can you evaluate whether the habits you've uncovered are truly supportive or not? The process of evaluation rests on an inquiry-based framework where curiosity collides with reflective questioning to determine the effects that your habitual patterns have on your life and achievements. The process makes space for you to evaluate the effectiveness of your habits and proactively determine what to do with them.

⇒ **Exercise #1b: Evaluate.** As you evaluate each uncovered habit, ask yourself the following questions (which can also be found on page 29 of your workbook):

- Does this habit contribute positively to who I am?
- Does this habit slow me down or get in the way of me achieving my goals?
- Would my future-self see this as a positive habit that is supporting our growth and development?
- Does this habit support the achievement of my vision?
- Is this habit in alignment with my values?
- What other parts of my day and routine are impacted by this habit? Does this habit set off a chain reaction? Are the impacts positive or negative?
- What are the impacts on my life if I modify, eliminate, or maintain this habit?
- Is there a new habit that could be integrated to better support my vision, values, and goals?

When Devon evaluated his habits, two specific insights arose for him. First, he realized his snooze button habit, which brought him temporary pleasure in the moment, was actually serving to negatively impact his morning routine while likely contributing to the perpetual sense of hurriedness he felt throughout the day.

Second, he suddenly felt quite confident that his employee-focused, flexible approach to scheduling was actually hurting his productivity and degrading his mental game while simultaneously setting a poor example for his team. He decided these were the top two habits he needed to address first.

Choose

Once you've uncovered your habits and evaluated the role they play in your life, the next step is to decide appropriate actions to take, if any. There are four options for consideration in this stage. You can **create** new habits, **modify** existing ones, **eliminate** unsupportive habits, or **maintain** those that serve you well. Here are some examples to make sense of these options:

> **Create:** You're interested in writing industry-relevant articles to share with your LinkedIn networks but have never ventured into this type of writing before. You decide to incorporate a new habit of writing for 30 minutes each morning before beginning your day. The consistency of the routine allows you to hone your writing skills while developing valuable content to share with your networks.
>
> **Modify:** You realize you're overly reliant on your habit of drinking caffeinated drinks throughout the day. You love jumpstarting your day with a hot cup of deliciously aromatic coffee and don't want to eliminate caffeine from your life completely, but you do want to reduce your overall intake. You decide to create a plan that addresses the cues, routine, and rewards of this habit, empowering you to slowly reduce your intake over the course of a few weeks.

Eliminate: Your post-dinner snacking habit is contributing to your expanding waistline and negatively impacting your ability to get a good night's sleep. You decide this habit needs to be eliminated altogether and begin substituting the routine portion of your habit loop with a different routine - a process we'll explore further in the coming pages. Now, when you're triggered to snack, you respond by drinking a glass of water and walking a few laps around your home.

Maintain: The first thing you do each morning is reach for your phone, grab your earbuds, and listen to a favorite song that gets you pumped and excited for the day ahead. This routine sets a positive, energetic tone for your day and is a supportive habit you want to continually maintain and foster. As a result, you make a conscious commitment to ensure this habit stays intact.

Deciding whether to create, modify, eliminate, or maintain your habits depends on how those particular habits serve you.

⇒ **Exercise #1c: Choose.** Space has been provided on page 30 of your workbook to explore this yourself. For Devon, he realized he needed to a) *eliminate* his unsupportive snooze button habit so he could intentionally create a more positive start to his day, and b) *modify* his current appointment scheduling approach so that he could better control the pace of his day instead of being controlled by it. With these decisions made, the next step was to apply the actions that would make these habit changes possible.

Apply

Once you've uncovered your habits, evaluated their effectiveness, and made a choice regarding how to proceed with those habits, the next step is to apply the necessary actions. For Devon, he stopped using his phone as an alarm and bought a traditional alarm clock, which he deliberately placed on a dresser on the far side of the room. When the alarm would sound (cue), he would physically get out of bed to turn it off (new routine) and found that padding his morning with these extra 18-minutes allowed him to start his day in a more calm, enjoyable manner (reward).

As an extension of this, Devon also found that he was less rushed when it came time to walk the dog, which made the experience far less frustrating for both of them. In addition, he discovered that having a bit of extra time to get the kids settled in for breakfast shifted the equation dramatically. As it turned out, the kids were taking their chaotic cues from him, not the other way around. Once the hurried nature of his approach was removed from the equation, the morning routine became more enjoyable for all, serving as a multilayered reward that continually reinforced his motivation and desire to maintain this new habit.

The next challenge Devon took on was adjusting his approach to appointment scheduling in an effort to regain control of his workday. His reflections during the *evaluation* phase made him realize that if he continued his habit of allowing others to dictate his schedule, he would never have the space required to be more proactive in his approach to business and life. But the right solution didn't immediately surface for him. This process required considerable trial and error. He had to experiment with different options to find a solution that a) worked for him personally, b) fit within his work environment, and c) was supportive of his team, who often relied on his assistance to close large sales transactions.

Knowing that a change to his personal scheduling habit would directly impact his team, he held a meeting to explain the challenge he was facing and invited their ideas for potentially resolving it. This gave his team the opportunity to explore the pros and cons of various solutions together, and to establish possible alternatives that could be considered and tested. The creativity that erupted from this brainstorming session gave Devon phenomenal ideas which he may not have unearthed on his own. In addition, the process gave him something even more important… the support, assistance, and permission from his team to make a change to a system that had long been in place, even though it had the potential to be initially disruptive.

After a bit of testing, a new system was eventually implemented which included designated time slots based on the type of appointment being scheduled. This new approach reduced the number of engagements Devon attended each day while providing space, both before and after, to prepare and debrief the progress of each client proposal.

The new solution achieved its primary goal of giving Devon breathing room throughout the day, which significantly decreased the cloud of stress that had loomed over his previously overpacked schedule. However, a secondary benefit surfaced for his team as well. With time allocated pre- and post-meetings to more thoroughly address client interactions, the length of the sales cycle was measurably shortened thanks to the insights that arose during these strategic sessions. The multiplicity of rewards served to strongly reinforce the new habit, and the approach taken toward incorporating his team to craft the solution set a new standard for collaboration and brainstorming.

It's easy to see how these habit and behavioral changes positively benefitted Devon, but let's explore how you can apply changes that propel your personal habits to work for you.

Making Habits Work for You

Though the 4-part process of uncovering, evaluating, choosing, and applying is theoretically easy, adjusting behaviors with enough consistency that they become habitual can be more of a challenge. This is partially because habits exist on a continuum ranging from deliberately mindful to thoughtlessly mindless, based on how long they've been in place.

Think of it this way, how much thought did you put into brushing your teeth this morning? Did you have to devote concentrated effort toward determining how to unscrew the toothpaste cap, or how to get the toothpaste out of the tube and onto the bristles? Did you have to expend energy trying to decide which hand would hold the toothbrush, which quadrant of your mouth you would start with, or which motions you would employ to thoroughly clean your teeth? Thankfully not, as this would be utterly exhausting. In circumstances like these, we can be grateful for well engrained habits that exist on the thoughtlessly mindless end of the spectrum.

However, the automaticity of this habit equally demonstrates how difficult it can be to modify or eliminate an aspect of our behavior that fully functions on autopilot. The less we have to think about a particular habit, the more concretely embedded the habitual pattern of behavior is, and the more highly resistant to change it can be. Try brushing your teeth with the opposite hand for thirty days and you'll quickly experience this challenge firsthand. Of course, it's easy to use the opposite hand when you're mindfully deliberate with your efforts, but what about when you wake up tired, find yourself rushed, or are forced to multitask? Layer in dimensions that compete for your mental attention and suddenly your previous habit returns to its long-established, prominent position.

Given the entrenched nature of existing habits, it's no surprise that a cycle of successes and setbacks line the habit formation journey. Thankfully, however, we don't have to be passive participants in this process. The balance of these cycles can be shifted in our favor when we understand the various factors that inhibit or promote behavioral change. Research published in the *Academy of Management Journal* points to three important factors in shifting this balance: 1) adjusting the environment, 2) attaching new habits to existing systems, and 3) focusing on small, incremental wins.[5] Let's explore each of these in more depth.

1. Adjusting the Environment

The role environment plays in habitual patterns of behavior is a widely researched area of study. As Marshall Goldsmith explores in *Triggers*, the environments we create for ourselves trigger certain behaviors which lead to the reinforcement of our habits.[6] If these habits support our growth and development, then the triggers can serve a beneficial role. However, if the habits in question negate our progress or achievement, then altering the environment to account for the triggers becomes essential.

As an example, a client recently shared her frustrations surrounding the consistent flow of interruptions she received throughout the day from people walking into her office to say hi and chit chat. She loved her colleagues and enjoyed being social, but this trend was impacting her productivity, causing her to take work home regularly, and negatively affecting her family life. After an hour of watching her behavior, the issue - and the solution - became obvious. She had a habit of smiling and waving at colleagues as they walked by and while she was just being her normal, friendly self, she didn't realize this very habit was the trigger (cue) that was drawing people into her office.

Telling someone who's warm and social by nature to change her friendly habits was not the solution - this would've only prompted cognitive dissonance. Instead, we turned her desk around so that it no longer faced the door and moved her most used files and supplies to a location where she could access them without turning her chair (routine). As people popped in to ask why the change, she politely shared that she was attempting to be more focused at work so that she could take less work home at night, making more time for her family.

People respected her "why" as well as her initiatives and supported her in this new endeavor. At first the change was difficult, because her habit of chatting with others had long been part of her routine and she genuinely enjoyed the socialization. But the shift in her environment made space for her to stay focused throughout the day, eliminating the previous stress that was attached to the stacks of work that she'd haul home each evening (reward).

Her experience is not an isolated or unique incident. As Benjamin Hardy extensively discusses in *Willpower Doesn't Work*, environment is the most critical factor in establishing healthy habits that empower us to achieve our goals.[7] When our environment is intentionally designed to support our goals and desires, we create an accelerated path toward making those dreams a reality. Create an environment that intentionally fosters good habits while making unsupportive ones inconvenient and you shift the balance in your favor. After all, you can't give in to your afternoon sweet tooth if unhealthy snacks no longer pad your pantry.

What environmental changes can you make to foster intentionally supportive habits?

⇒ **Exercise#2:** Using the space provided on page 31 of your workbook, make a list of the various environments you find yourself regularly surrounded by (home, work, airplane/car, gym, etc). Which aspects of these environments beneficially support the positive habits you seek to perpetually practice? Which aspects negatively reinforce bad habits you endeavor to modify or eliminate? What can you add to your environment(s) to make them more supportive? What can you remove from your environment(s) to make them less distracting?

Don't limit yourself with this activity. Take time to explore your environments and their resulting impacts from multiple angles, then apply a bit of creativity to the process. Sometimes, it's the simplest adjustments that lead to the biggest benefits so employ your Curiosity and Creativity strengths and have a bit of fun with the process. Some examples from past clients include:

- Putting a reversible sign on an office door to indicate when interruptions are welcome versus when focused thought is taking place.
- No longer carrying cash, making afternoon trips to the breakroom snack machine a thing of the past.
- Replacing artwork with a white board that keeps goals and plans visibly front and center each day.
- Having an email autoresponder that notifies others of your new process for only checking email twice daily, at 9 am and 3 pm.
- Purchasing file cabinets so that paper clutter is eliminated, files are organized, and time is no longer wasted searching for that one document.
- Keeping learning materials (such as audio books and industry-related podcasts) on your phone so that travel time becomes learning time.
- Adding a diffuser to your office that fills your environment with a positive, calming scent.
- Putting a countdown timer in your office to maintain concentrated effort during blocks of focused work time.

2. New Habits and Existing Systems

In chapter one we learned that the pathway to freedom is lined with systems. We explored how our lives are made up of a series of interconnected systems that, when deliberately designed and intentionally crafted, pave a pathway to our desired outcomes. However, when systems are allowed to operate by default, the accompanying results are often haphazard and inconsistent. Recognizing the specific systems that operate within our lives and identifying the various elements that help or hinder our progress is essential to bringing our future vision to fruition.

As Donella Meadows explores in *Thinking in Systems: A Primer*, learning to recognize our behavioral patterns is an important part of the process.

Doing so gives us empowering insights into how our habits and behaviors impact our overall systems.[8] Adjusting behaviors to improve the efficiency of a system becomes paramount when we realize that our habit loops are a series of individual yet deeply connected systems. Duhigg brings this point to life in *The Power of Habit* when he explores the research behind adjusting the routine within a habit loop while maintaining the originating cue.[9]

To put this into context, the scent of piping hot, fresh donuts wafting through a morning meeting no longer derails my health and fitness goals because I consciously crafted a new routine in response to an existing cue; smell the donuts, grab the ONE bar. This approach requires less effort than designing a completely new habit loop, while simultaneously increasing my ability to effectively change my previously unsupportive habit.

Another means for tying new behaviors to existing systems is through behavior bundling, a concept explored by James Clear in *Atomic Habits*.[10] With this approach, you intertwine desirable habits with behaviors that already bring you joy and fill you with positive emotions (rewards).

As an example, let's say you have a favorite Netflix series that consistently puts a smile on your face *and* you're trying to develop a habit of going to the gym four times a week. Combine your existing Netflix habit with your fitness goals by only allowing yourself to watch the series when you're on cardio equipment at the gym. By tying these two habits together, it heightens the rewards for both activities while driving intrinsic motivation for the desired habit that you're working to develop.

Similarly, you can also leverage the power of habit stacking, a process where new habits are triggered by, and integrated into, existing habit loops.[11,12] In this instance, you evaluate habitual patterns of behavior that are well engrained and occur on autopilot, then stack an additional habit within the framework of the existing routine.

To picture this in action, let's say that after you eat breakfast each day (cue), the first thing you do is brush your teeth (routine), leaving you with fresh breath and a sparkling smile to start the day (reward). Since brushing your teeth after breakfast is a habitual practice that takes place without much thought or effort, stacking an additional habit within the framework of this existing habit loop can simplify the process of incorporating new behaviors. Let's say you want to incorporate a new fitness activity into your existing teeth-brushing routine. Perhaps the revised habit-stacked loop would include eating breakfast (cue), brushing your teeth *and* doing 20 squats (routine), and enjoying a great smile *and* buns of steel (rewards).

⇒ **Exercise #3: Enhancing Your Systems.** Revisiting the habits you've uncovered and the environments they exist in, explore the potential for incorporating new habits into your existing systems. How can you leverage 'behavior bundling', 'habit stacking', or 'swapping the routine' to improve your systems? Use the worksheet on page 32 of your workbook to explore the potential benefits of such system changes.

When we begin evaluating the role our habits and behaviors play within the context of our systems, it's easy to see the impacts they have on the achievement of our goals and dreams. Our habits are part of our systems, but systems don't exist in a vacuum; everything is interrelated. Take this connectedness into account by designing systems that are intentionally crafted to support your future self. When you do so, your systems will begin to work in conjunction with one another and in support of your bigger vision.

3. Small, Incremental Wins

The third important factor in promoting positive habit change is to keep your efforts bite-sized and achievable. Habit change isn't about swinging for the fences or scoring home runs; it's about small, incremental wins that equate to big victories over time. It's the difference between committing to a behavior that feels potentially daunting and overwhelming, such as reading fifty business books per year, versus committing to a more attainable habit, such as reading five pages per day. Despite what the commercials might have one believe, I've never met anyone who lost 50 lbs. overnight. Though I've met plenty of people who made simple alterations to their eating habits, lost 1 - 2 lbs. per week, and found themselves 50 lbs. lighter over the course of a year. Small wins, by definition of what they are, are always within striking distance. The question becomes, are your systems deliberately designed to help you achieve the small wins that will add up to big victories over time?

Often, small wins are much smaller than we even realize. Developing a habit of jogging doesn't start with a 5-mile run, it starts with putting on running shoes. Backing this up further, putting on running shoes may start with setting them by your bedroom door the night before (cue), triggering you to put them on before leaving your bedroom in the morning (routine). Once the shoes are on, the smallest win has been achieved, making a person more likely to take the next step, and the next and the next, until they're jogging down the street. When we focus on the tiny, incremental wins that make behavior change more likely, we leave space to naturally develop empowering habits that support our long-term growth.

Research conducted by Stanford University researcher and professor BJ Fogg has revealed that when we take on too much at one time and upend our lives in pursuit of habit change, it actually causes motivation to plummet.[13] Once motivation wanes, we become overwhelmed by the big changes we initially sought to implement, causing us to give up on our positive intentions and return to our previous habits, even if those habits are unhelpful and stand between us and our goals. Small steps and simple wins may not initially feel like they'll lead to massive shifts in achievement but they're the key to unlocking meaningful behavior change that sticks.

Are your systems built on a foundation of small wins that lead to big successes? What adjustments can you make to leverage consistent wins that support powerful habits?

While adjusting the environment, attaching new habits to existing systems, and focusing on small, incremental wins are essential to developing successful behaviors that support the achievement of your vision and goals, it's important to note that habits are not one-size-fits-all. There is no single solution or prescribed set of habits that will propel you to success. However, when you reflect on the habits and behaviors that contribute most to your growth and development, while also identifying those that act as roadblocks to success, you can begin making adjustments that support your vivid vision.

Put another way, adopt the habits and behaviors of your future self and a path to your vision unfolds before you. As Gretchen Rubin remarks in *Better Than Before*, "In many ways, our habits are our destiny. And changing our habits allows us to alter that destiny".[14] But are all habits created equal?

Cornerstone Habits

Historically, a cornerstone was the first stone set during the building process. Stonemasons took great care in measuring and cutting this stone, understanding the critical role it played in supporting and aligning the dwelling as a whole. If effort and artistry were lacking and the cornerstone was not perfectly squared, the stones extending from the left and right would be askew, leaving the building out of alignment. Furthermore, if the cornerstone were not a structurally sound stone, it risked being incapable of supporting the weight of the stones placed upon it, putting the integrity of the entire building in jeopardy.

While advancements in architecture have rendered cornerstones immaterial as they no longer play a critical role in the structural soundness of the building process, the concept of cornerstones has great applicability when filtered through the lens of habit formation. Not all habits are created equal; some are more important, some less. When we identify and connect with the cornerstone habits that play an elevated role in our personal systems, we can fast track our journey toward bringing our vision to life. This concept is all about leverage. In other words, what are the cornerstone habits that directly support or influence additional habits, elevating your efforts along the way?

As an example, a research study conducted in the field of neuroscience sought to explore the structural brain changes that take place in individuals who meditate.[15] Using functional neuroimaging technology, images of brain activity in meditators and non-meditators were captured. The research highlighted eight different brain regions that are altered through meditation, demonstrating that mindfulness meditation "involves multiple aspects of mental function that use multiple complex interactive networks in the brain".[16] The effects of these results showed that those who engaged in a mindfulness meditation practice had enhanced attention control, improved emotion regulation, and heightened self-awareness, all of which contributed to a reduction in stress and an increase in well-being.[17]

One benefit of enhanced attention control is that it enables a person to maintain deeper focus for longer periods of time. With improved emotion regulation, one can reduce stress and anxiety while maintaining better control over emotional reactions. With heightened self-awareness, one can be mindful of their thoughts, feelings, actions, and behaviors at a deeper, more conscious level, empowering them to make better decisions that are in alignment with their vision and values. In other words, meditation is a cornerstone habit whose benefits multiply, supporting a wider swath of positive behaviors that lead to the achievement of one's goals.

As the above example affirms, not all habits are created equal. Some habits, by their very nature, can spark a chain reaction that reinforces and supports other habits. Deliberately and selectively leveraging cornerstone habits simplifies the process of achieving your vivid vision and living into your future self. While there are several habits that can act in this capacity, here are a few specific examples that can be incorporated to boost overall success:

- **Build Your Willpower Muscle:** A 2005 University of Pennsylvania study revealed that students who were high in self-discipline consistently outperformed those with higher IQs.[18] Additionally, the study showed that self-discipline accounted for more than twice as much variance as IQ in final grades, highlighting the finding that failure to exercise self-discipline is a major reason why individuals fall short of their intellectual potential. Building willpower and self-discipline as cornerstone habits increases your ability to overcome the challenges and hurdles that test your resolve.

- **Get Out and Get Physical:** The brain-body connection is nothing new - a plethora of research detailing dozens of benefits has long been studied and documented. However, the neurological benefits afforded by exercise don't get nearly the credit they deserve for serving as an incredibly powerful cornerstone habit. As one research study detailed, subjects who exercised regularly were found to have increased levels of brain-derived neurotrophic factor (BDNF), a powerful protein that supports the growth and development of new brain cells, promotes brain health, and improves cognitive performance.[19] Strengthen your brain by increasing your BDNF production through exercise and you'll find that you have more brainpower for implementing supportive habits that lead to the achievement of your goals.

- **Prioritize a Sleep Schedule:** Research has repeatedly shown that sleep deprivation negatively impacts cognitive performance. As one example, research published in *Nature Neuroscience* highlighted the finding that even mild sleep disruptions impact hippocampal activity, leading to degraded memory performance in healthy adults.[20] A separate study published in *Frontiers in Neurology* demonstrated how sleep acts to renormalize synaptic strength in our brains, restoring cellular homeostasis and resulting in the beneficial consolidation and integration of both procedural and declarative memories.[21] In other words, sleep helps us remember and retain more of what we learn and experience. These findings highlight the important role sleeps plays in brain health and cognitive functioning, showcasing sleep's status as a cornerstone habit.

- **Master the Art of Goal Achievement:** Thousands of studies surrounding the many benefits of goal setting have been conducted over the years. Repeatedly, the research has shown that goal setting increases self-efficacy, enhances motivation, improves agency, inspires higher levels of perseverance, enhances effort and performance, and leads to the development of increasingly more difficult goals, which supports further expansion of all the previously noted benefits. Goal setting, and mastering the art of goal achievement, is a critical cornerstone habit, and one that will be explored at length in chapters eight and nine.

- **Make Your Bed:** While Admiral McRaven's 2014 University of Texas commencement speech and subsequent book popularized the notion of starting each day by making your bed, the reasons for doing so are scientifically sound. Firstly, it brings you that initial "small win" of the day while reinforcing the value in the little things; how you treat the smaller details in life sets the tone for how you approach bigger aspects. Everything matters. Additionally, consistently taking action on small, positive habits which generate immediate rewards improves self-efficacy while driving motivation and perseverance toward other habits where the rewards may not be as quickly evident, such as the delay between altering eating habits and losing weight. It's not really about the bed after all, it's about the psychological processes that are activated *because* you made your bed.

- **Practice an Attitude of Gratitude:** Setting aside a few minutes each day to engage in a deliberate gratitude practice provides a variety of benefits. As research in the field of neuroscience has shown, when our thoughts and attention are focused on that which we're grateful for (people, places, experiences, objects, relationships, etc.), our brains respond by stimulating positive neurotransmitters, such as dopamine and serotonin, which anchor us in the PEA and promotes feelings of happiness, joy, and contentedness.[22,23] Experiencing these feelings fuels our positive emotions, which in turn influences our actions, reactions, and perceptions. Start your day rooted in positive emotions and your ability to see the glass as half full increases, driving intrinsic motivation as you go.

In each of the above cases, these cornerstone habits act as catalysts to growth, prompting the meaningful support and development of other habits and behaviors that exist within your system. However, as with anything, determining which cornerstone habits provide the most leverage for your particular situation is an important part of the equation. In the next chapter, we'll explore how to be your own experiment and identify the cornerstone habits that will serve you and your future self best.

chapter seven

The Experiment of You

"Do not be too timid and squeamish about your actions. All life is an experiment. The more experiments you make the better."

- Ralph Waldo Emerson

Sheryl's Story cont.

When Sheryl, whom we met at the beginning of the last chapter, first received Chuck's feedback, she was uncertain how to proceed. She understood the merit of his words but struggled to conceptually apply them. After all, the habits that comprised her patterns of behavior weren't negative habits. In fact, they had led to the successes that she and her team regularly experienced. She was proud of who she was and what she'd accomplished but she also recognized the complacency she'd inadvertently developed along the way.

Her achievements were limited to the safe confines of an environment she'd worked diligently to cultivate. As she reflected on the safe, protective bubble she'd unwittingly built for herself, she suddenly realized how spot-on Chuck's feedback was. If she didn't develop habits and behaviors that would challenge her to grow beyond her current comfort zone, she'd remain locked in place with promotion opportunities perpetually out of reach.

Given that she and Chuck shared a meaningful conversation the week before and knowing that her organization had an open-door policy that encouraged dialogue, she decided to schedule a 15-minute meeting with

Chuck. She hoped he could share specific instructions on how to move forward, perhaps a recipe for growth and development that, if followed, would push her beyond the boundaries of her comfort zone. She desperately craved a step-by-step manual that would walk her through each aspect of the process but what she received was anything but.

Chuck was excited to see that Sheryl had taken the initiative to schedule a meeting with him. He listened intently as she shared her gratitude for their chance encounter and detailed the meaningful insights that had surfaced for her since. She acknowledged how her actions and behaviors had created an environment where she shined with ease, always playing it safe within her comfort zone. And while these acknowledgements were easy for her to come by, she also expressed the challenges she was facing in determining how to shift her equation. Chuck nodded in agreement, shared a few words of affirmation, then opened his desk drawer and pulled out a stack of business cards. He shuffled through the cards until he found the exact one he was looking for, then pushed it across the desk to Sheryl.

"Give this woman a call and let her know I suggested you reach out. She runs a women's leadership networking group that you may find beneficial". With that, Chuck closed the meeting but not before telling Sheryl that he was glad she reached out and looked forward to seeing what surfaced for her. Sheryl left his office feeling a bit unsettled. After all, that wasn't the step-by-step recipe she was hoping for. In fact, the exchange felt a bit anticlimactic, especially after the dynamic conversation they previously had, but she decided to trust his instincts and make the call… a call that would change the trajectory of her life and put her on a different path to achievement.

The Experiment of You

Everyone is on their own journey, with different experiences, knowledge sets, opinions, and ideas that come together to form who they are and how they experience the world. For this reason, there is no standard prescription for constructing a set of habits or behaviors that best support the successful achievement of one's goals. What works for one may not work for another but the *process* of discovering what propels an individual to thrive is the same for us all. *The key is to be your own experiment.*

Just as Thomas Edison experimented with different filaments until he created the modern-day lightbulb, each of us must engage in a process of trial and error if we are to determine the unique combination of habits that pave the pathway to our individual success. However, just as Edison is rumored to have had 10,000 failures before discovering the final solution, we must embrace the reality that experimentation rarely results in the right solution the first time. It's up to each of us to test and retest a variety of approaches, embracing any hiccups or failures with a growth mindset, and refining our results until our experiments produce a working solution.

There are variety of ways you can experiment with habits and behaviors to find your winning combination. It all starts with a) leveraging the exercises you completed in the previous chapters (so make sure you have your workbook handy) and b) applying any or all of the experimental protocols that follow. Like Edison, it's only through testing, adjusting, and retesting that you'll have your lightbulb moments and discover your personalized recipe for habit success.

1. Act, Reflect, Inquire, Repeat: Launching from a foundation of inquiry, engage in a perpetual cycle of action and reflection. Begin by asking yourself where you can take action to create, modify, or eliminate habits or behaviors in better support of your future self (your answers to this first step are captured in the workbook pages from the previous chapter). Next, set a window of time to test the action you're taking; this is your "experimentation" phase. As you're conducting your experiment, record your results daily, taking note of what worked and what didn't, and noting any emotional responses you may have had along the way. As examples, clients often share having felt a deep sense of contentedness when they begin a gratitude practice, as well as a heightened sense of motivation when they align their goals with their vivid vision.

When your experimentation window closes, reflect on your results to determine what additional adjustments can or should be made in the pursuit of finding your most supportive solution. During this process of reflection, deepen your inquiry by asking yourself more and more questions until you unearth tailored solutions that drive you toward your goals. Sometimes this can be as simple as questioning and testing if a certain habit would serve you better at a different time of day, or as complex as determining if drastic changes need to be made to your social circle. You won't know what truly makes you flourish until you deepen your inquiry and test what surfaces.

⇒ **Exercise #1:** There's a worksheet available on page 33 of your workbook to help you implement this first experiment.

2. Advance Planning Improves Outcomes: Some habits are more challenging to release than others. Experimenting with how to overcome these can be hugely empowering. When we know we're apt to give in to certain behaviors, creating an action plan in advance can go a long way towards improving our outcomes. In *Atomic Habits,* James Clear speaks to these proactive aims as "implementation intentions"; thoughtfully constructed plans that anticipate challenges in advance and equip an individual to successfully overcome impending hurdles.[1]

The most effective solution I've found for designing and implementing these plans is to follow if/then logic and power it with a bigger why. My favorite equation for doing so is "When I / I will / So I". As an example, let's say I'm trying to eliminate my habit of mindless snacking.

When I... head to the pantry for a snack,
I will... drink a glass of water and wait three minutes before eating anything,
So I... give myself time to overcome the craving and feel stronger in how my choices connect with my health goals.

The "**When I**" is the triggering event or cue that currently leads to a particular habit. The "**I will**" is your plan of action; a personal commitment you are making to yourself and your future success. Lastly, the "**So I**" is your why and is tied to the feeling you get when you succeed.

⇒ **Exercise #2:** Included on page 34 of your workbook is a simple worksheet to support you in designing implementation plans for overcoming unsupportive habits.

3. Let Go to Let In: Some habits have opposing forces that work in tandem to keep them firmly locked in place. If effort is exerted on trying to strengthen the positive side of the equation without releasing the negative side, it can result in a challenging impasse that entrenches the unsupportive habit even more deeply. As an example, in order to develop patience, one must let go of impatience. However, the process of developing patience versus that of releasing impatience can look very different in practice. If efforts are devoted toward mindfully observing patience throughout the day, it's easy to get caught up in the flow of life and lose track of the goal. On the other hand, if the focus is instead placed on releasing impatience whenever it arises, you now have a natural cue and can create a habit loop (cue, routine, reward) that supports the release of impatience as a method for developing patience. While the end result is the same - patience is being developed - the path to achievement is quite different.

⇒ **Exercise #3:** Looking at the habits you uncovered in the previous chapter, are there any that require you to release its opposing force in order to shift the pattern? What type of habit loop can you create in support of releasing the opposing behavior? Space to explore and journal about this has been provided on page 35 of your workbook.

4. Accountability Drives Motivation: Accountability can come in all shapes and sizes, from habit trackers to mentors to gamified apps - the options are endless as are the benefits. Layering accountability into the equation leads to greater motivation, more consistent results, quicker development of supportive habits, increased self-efficacy, and heightened confidence. The key lies with experimenting to determine which forms of accountability work best for you and how you can build them into your existing system. A few examples include:

- Connecting with a friend who holds similar health goals to act as one another's accountability partners.
- Leveraging an app like HabitShare, which enables you and a partner to declare, then track, one another's progress toward implementing better habits and behaviors.
- Hiring a coach to help you elevate your habits and take your efforts to the next level.
- Joining a mastermind group that holds everyone accountable to ongoing growth, development, and goal achievement.
- Using a printed calendar that's kept in a visibly obvious place to track the efforts surrounding the development of a daily habit.
- Maintaining a food journal to track your eating habits and improve your health outcomes.

⇒ **Exercise #4:** Returning to your workbook and looking at the habits you uncovered in the previous chapter, which habits or behaviors would potentially benefit from accountability? What types of accountability systems would serve you best? How can you test various methods of accountability to determine which would provide the strongest results? Who can you trust and rely on to help hold you accountable to the habits of your future self? Use the space provided on page 36 of your workbook to help you develop accountability plans.

5. Routines Accelerate Results: Routines are a proven method for developing and enhancing supportive habits that skyrocket your success. Combining a series of habits into a singular routine allows you to simplify the habit loop while reaping a variety of benefits. As an example, when multiple supportive habits are integrated into a cohesive, integrated routine, which is then prompted by a single cue, it becomes easier to consistently practice those individual habits due to their linked nature. Examples of beneficial routines that can become sources of experimentation include:

- Morning routines that incorporate physical, mental, and spiritual health, setting a positive tone for your day.
- Evening routines that support better sleep habits and lead to increased energy levels over time.
- Focused work block routines that spark your creativity and empower you to produce your best work.
- Commuting routines that empower a stress-free transition from work mode to partner or family mode, creating mental space for quality time with your loved ones.

Remember, structure is freedom. Routines allow you to create supportive systems that work interdependently to drive positive results in a variety of areas. When crafted with intentionality and care, they can supercharge your cornerstone habits and fast track your results.

⇒ **Exercise #5:** See page 37 in your workbook to develop powerful routines of your own.

TIP: Enlist Your Signature Strengths. As you experiment with different approaches to habit development, explore which of your signature strengths can be leveraged to accelerate your results. Since signature strengths are those which come most naturally to us, this approach often becomes the key to unlocking new solutions in a more simplistic and fun fashion because the approach complements who we are at our core.

As an example, if you want to develop a learning habit that expands your industry-related knowledge and Perseverance is one of your signature strengths, you can intentionally create learning-oriented tasks that build upon one another to achieve this goal. With the knowledge that Perseverance leads to a natural orientation toward task-completion and creates a cycle of incremental achievement while enhancing self-efficacy, one can amplify their results while minimizing their efforts. Put simply, signature strengths can become the activation energy that accelerates the formation of new habits.

Leveraging Habits to Shape Goal Achievement

Goals and dreams aren't magically wished into existence; they take hard work and persistent action. They require us to act in ways that are consistent with our future selves, yet this alone does not guarantee success - it's only part of the equation. Supportive habits, once established, become the foundation that supports larger goal achievement. With clarity established surrounding the behaviors you're creating, modifying, eliminating, and maintaining to support your growth and development, the next step is to master the art and science of goal setting, empowering you to bring your vivid vision to life.

But before we move on to the next chapter, it's important to note that adjusting and altering habits to improve your life and achieve your goals isn't a one-time event. It's a perpetual process of learning, discovery, and experimentation. When we understand our habits and identify the ways in which they contribute or detract from our bigger vision, we can make powerful course corrections that pave our way to success. In addition, as our life circumstances change and we achieve various goals on the path to our vision, we may realize that certain habits or routines no longer serve us as well as they once did. This is natural and to be expected. In the same way that one bath won't keep you clean for life, one exploration into your habits and behaviors won't last forever either. But the good news is, you now have the tools and resources to revisit your habits and make changes whenever necessary.

Sheryl's exploration into the habits and behaviors that created her outcomes led to several revelations. For one, she realized it was possible to have habits that were paradoxically helpful and hindering at the same time. As an example, her habit of working hard on her departmental goals was beneficial in one regard, but the narrowed approach failed to consider additional corporate or personal goals, contributing significantly to her stagnation. Learning how to broaden this habit so that it encompassed her personal *and* professional life became central to her development.

She also realized that while she had developed a strong skill set specific to her role, general learning was not part of her equation. Without continually absorbing new knowledge and perspectives to round out her value, she realized she would continue feeling ill-equipped to contribute in larger ways. Additionally, she recognized how her pattern of passivity towards her growth and development bubbled over into multiple areas of life, creating a comfort zone that was far bigger than she'd ever acknowledged. While she was initially unsure of how Chuck's recommendation to join a women's leadership group would help address any of these challenges, she soon learned it was exactly the solution she needed.

The networking aspect of the group led to new connections and relationships with women in similar positions who had faced related challenges. Through connection and dialogue, Sheryl was able to gain insights and perspectives on how others overcame their hurdles, which empowered her to find solutions of her own. When she got more comfortable with the group and began sharing how she struggled to move beyond her comfort zone, they challenged her to push through her boundaries by presenting a segment about the limiting structures of comfort zones at one of the upcoming meetings. She reluctantly agreed and was terrified at the prospect but found herself inspired and elated after having met the challenge with energy and zeal. She was blossoming in beautiful ways, and her growth had only just begun.

Her interaction with the group led to her connecting with a leadership coach, who helped her hone her communication and negotiation skills, further building up the confidence she needed to take on more challenges. In addition, a learning plan was developed empowering Sheryl to expand her knowledge base across a wide variety of subjects. Suddenly, she started seeing unexpected connections across various disciplines, which led to a renewed sense of creativity and innovation when approaching workplace challenges.

It took a year of showing up and playing bigger than ever before, but her efforts were eventually noticed throughout the senior ranks of the organization. Her personal commitment to growth and development collided with the company's passionate initiative to shift toward becoming a learning organization - a transformation that required them to identify a change agent who embraced learning and was capable of spearheading the efforts. While it was Chuck who initially threw Sheryl's name in the ring, it didn't take long for consensus among the executive ranks to secure her future opportunity.

Sheryl had shed her pattern of passivity, burst beyond the boundaries of her comfort zone, established powerfully supportive habits, and confidently stepped into her new role as the company's Chief Learning Officer, a position that allowed her to live into her desire to make a bigger difference within the organization. With her attention and efforts now directed toward launching a new corporate initiative, creating a vision for the role and crafting a concrete goal plan to implement it became her primary focus.

part three

Achieving Your Goals

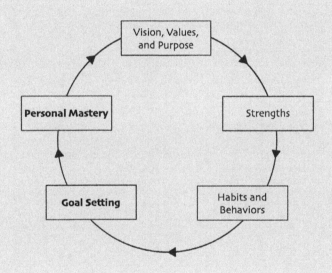

chapter eight

The Art & Science of Goal Setting

"Always remember, your focus determines your reality."

- George Lucas

Where the Rubber Meets the Road

There are no shortcuts to success. Someone who doesn't see merit in exploring their values, connecting with and physically writing down their visions, discovering and intentionally leveraging their strengths, and focusing time and energy on developing supportive habits *prior* to crafting and pursuing their goals, will continue to be met with unnecessary obstacles. Their approach will keep them locked in the same patterns of behavior that created the frustrations they're currently trying to escape.

Solving this challenge was front and center when I designed this program, which is why the system is constructed as it is. It's purpose-built to develop the leader within, creating a solid foundation that supports the pursuit and achievement of one's bigger goals and dreams. I share this because it's important to acknowledge and celebrate the steps you've taken thus far.

Kudos to you for putting in the hard work, completing the previous exercises, and getting to this point. The ease with which you'll now be able to define and achieve goals that are in alignment with your vision and values will be monumentally rewarding. Additionally, you're now living into your future self - a person who's capable of achieving the vivid vision you've set your sights on. With that, it's time for the rubber to meet the road as we dive into the art and science of goal setting.

The Science of Goal Setting

Just as we learned that not all habits are created equal, the same is true of the goals we set for ourselves. Some goals can feel important in the moment, but when contrasted against our vision we realize they're sucking us into an empty void of busy work that doesn't positively contribute to our bigger picture. On the flip side, when goals are intentionally designed to support our compelling vision they can be worth their weight in gold, generating significant leverage and propelling us toward the finish line faster.

Dan was experiencing the former phenomenon on a daily basis. He spent hours each day on social media marketing because he believed this was the best way to grow his business and brand. The problem was that his content creation efforts weren't focused or purposeful. Without clarity surrounding where his video photography business would be in five years, his daily activities were devoted to creating content that was fun to look at but didn't contribute to measurable business growth. In other words, Dan was always busy but rarely productive in revenue-generating ways. This equation shifted drastically when he focused on the long-term growth of his brand, crafted a detailed five-year strategy for his business, and built a goal plan to bring his vision to reality.

Creating a vision-based goal plan ensures that the nitty-gritty action steps taken on a daily basis are intentionally and incrementally moving you closer toward your future vision. When actions are in alignment with the bigger picture, you're able to fast-track your efforts and accelerate your results. It's the difference between meandering about until you haphazardly happen upon your destination or mapping the route in advance to ensure a more direct, efficient, and purposeful approach.

While all our efforts up to this point have STRENGTHENED us to become the person capable of bringing our vivid vision to life, goal setting is the necessary ingredient for taking action and making big things happen. After all, one can have the best laid ideas in the world, but without specific goals to make those ideas a reality, nothing will come of it.

Goal setting may seem as simple as creating a target and taking action to achieve it, but that approach often produces hollow goals devoid of the intention and leverage necessary to produce big results. To understand why, it helps to review some of the psychological underpinnings of goal setting. As the research has repeatedly shown, properly constructed, meaningful goals have a direct impact on performance in three powerful ways:

1. They direct attention and effort toward goal-relevant activities and, perhaps more importantly, AWAY from goal-irrelevant activities.[1] In other words, vision-based goals become a relevancy filter that prevent you from wasting time, effort, and energy in areas that won't advance your cause.

2. They have an energizing function that continually serves to motivate the ongoing pursuit of additional goal-specific tasks and activities.[2] When you experience consistent progress toward the bigger picture it creates a perpetual cycle of goal pursuit and attainment, positively enhancing persistence and perseverance, and resulting in increased fortitude and drive.[3] This cycle reduces the likelihood that you'll give up before hitting the finish line.

3. They expand your skills and know-how, resulting in an increase in task-relevant knowledge and strategies. This, in turn, leads to an increase in self-efficacy, which further fuels your ability to commit to, and attain, larger, more complex goals.[4,5]

Gary Latham and Edwin Locke studied the science of goal setting in individual and organizational contexts for decades. Among their many valuable findings was the research-backed notion that "specific difficult goals plus high self-efficacy for attaining them are the impetus for high performance".[6] As their research amplified, when goals are constructed in a certain way and take particular aspects into account, they feed into the "High-Performance Cycle", turbocharging the results achieved.[7]

- The High Performance Cycle starts with high, challenging goals;
- High goals lead to high performance;
- These, in turn, lead to the achievement of rewards;
- Which increases satisfaction;
- Which leads to increased confidence and self-efficacy;
- Prompting a new set of challenging goals.

Thankfully, designing goal plans which naturally embody the elements that spark the High-Performance Cycle is not overly challenging or complex. Once you know the tenets of a strong and effective goal, developing detailed goal plans that guide you on your journey toward making your vision a reality becomes far easier.

There are seven main aspects that lead to optimal goal achievement and success:

#1 Personally Meaningful

The first key is to ensure that your goals are personally meaningful. Far too often, people miss this step and wind up with goals that resemble meaningless to-dos instead of strategic initiatives. We saw this with Dan earlier in this chapter. When your goals don't excite and invigorate you, when they aren't driving you towards fulfilling your dreams and achieving your vision, they can begin to feel heavy, exhausting, and demotivating. However, inspiring goals that pull you out of bed in the morning put your goal-setting superpower in hyperdrive. But what exactly makes a goal *meaningful*? The scientific community has defined meaningful goals as those which are in alignment with, and in support of, a person's beliefs, morals, and values. This is why we began our journey by focusing on our vision and values. With those in place, personally meaningful goals can naturally surface.

#2 Goal Commitment

As an extension of the first point, research has shown that when an individual pursues personally meaningful goals, their intrinsic motivation increases, empowering them to persist longer in the face of challenge.[8,9] When commitment is naturally heightened, we become more resilient in the face of setbacks, viewing each failure as a learning opportunity and adjusting our approach accordingly.[10] In essence, high commitment makes space for failure to serve as a feedback mechanism, which sparks our growth mindset and provides insights as to where we're off track and what adjustments need to be made. Taking action on the insights uncovered by the feedback creates a success loop which further propels us closer to the achievement of our larger goals, continuing to drive motivation and persistence in the process. The net-net: a deeply personal connection to a goal keeps us in the fight.

#3 Temporal Proximity

Temporal proximity, meaning the timeframe associated with a particular goal, is a well-researched aspect of goal setting and goal achievement. As the research has shown, the combination of proximal (near- and medium-term) goals and distal (long-term) goals results in better performance than distal goals alone.[11] Why is this the case?

- For one, short-term goals provide a means of measuring progress toward long-term goals. This creates a feedback loop that allows for course correction when it appears the distal goal may be missed.
- Second, proximal goals inherently contain shorter-frame deadlines. This infuses an innate sense of urgency that, in turn, reduces procrastination and increases goal-directed action.
- Third, proximal goals enhance self-efficacy for achieving the distal goal. In other words, baby steps on smaller goals increase one's belief that they can achieve their larger, overarching goals. This serves to increase persistence and effort on both proximal and distal goal levels.
- And fourth, proximal goals have a direct impact on motivation, performance, and achievement. As we make progress on our vision-based, short-term goals, the path to our larger goals crystallizes before us, propelling our success.

#4 Accountability

Dr. Gail Matthews, a psychology professor at Dominican University in California, conducted an in-depth workplace goal study. Her research revealed that those who 1) physically wrote down their goals, 2) committed to goal-direction actions, and 3) had an accountability system in place that included sending weekly updates to an accountability partner, saw a 70% success rate in goal achievement.[12] This was double the success rate of the group who simply *thought* about their goals but didn't have any accountability systems in place.

As her research showcased, when there's an expectation to report your progress to someone else, you're less likely to procrastinate and more motivated to push through.[13] Additionally, there's a sense of pride in sharing your goal-directed achievements with a trusted partner, which also sparks the PEA and drives motivation. Accountability can come in a few different forms, including both self-accountability and partner-based, but the results are amplified when the two approaches are blended.

Self-accountability:
1) Use a daily planner
2) Rate your daily performance
3) Review your progress weekly
4) Keep a habit tracker

Partner-based accountability:
1) Hire a coach
2) Find a mentor
3) Join a mastermind
4) Get an accountability partner

#5 Daily Action

Goals take time to achieve. The bigger and more audacious your vision, the more goals and subgoals your plan will include, and naturally, the longer it will take to bring to fruition. However, by outlining short-, medium- and long-term goals, having target dates for completion, and taking *daily* action on subgoals, the process becomes manageable, attainable, and enjoyable. Taking daily action on goal-specific tasks keeps you in a state of momentum, continually driving motivation, persistence, and achievement while simultaneously preventing goal irrelevant activities from pervading your calendar.

#6 SMART Goals

You may already be familiar with "SMART" goals, but what you may not know is that the SMART goal structure has been studied, measured, and tested extensively across a variety of research-based disciplines, including the psychological sciences. The reason the acronym has become so commonplace is because of the research-backed validity of its individual components. Those components include goals that are:

- **Specific**: Vague goals yield vague results. Purposeful goals that rest on a foundation of specificity empower you to take meaningful action toward consistent achievement.
- **Measurable**: You can't manage what you don't measure. Ensuring your goals include a measurable component allows you to evaluate if you've successfully met your objectives.
- **Attainable**: The strongest goals are those that are challenging yet attainable. Multiple studies have shown that difficult goals, as opposed to easy ones, propel an individual toward achievement by motivating extra effort and driving persistence.[14,15,16]
- **Relevant**: SMART goals are relevant to the bigger picture. They keep us focused on the activities that promote the achievement of our vision while preventing distractions from derailing our efforts.
- **Time-Bound**: Goals without deadlines are nothing more than a wish. SMART goals include a specific deadline, which serves as a driver for completion.

In addition to provoking the High Performance Cycle, research has also shown that SMART goals, by their very nature, 1) decrease habits of procrastination, 2) increase well-being, 3) decrease stress and anxiety, 4) increase self-efficacy, 5) increase life satisfaction, and 6) reduce barriers caused by perfectionism. In other words, SMART goals are high-octane super fuel for your goal getting efforts.

What does a SMART goal look like in action? Here are a few examples to help bring the SMART framework to life.

Sales Management Goal

- Poor Goal: I'll increase team sales numbers over last month.
- SMART Goal: I will increase our team sales numbers from 20 transactions last month to 25 transactions next month, through the implementation of two focus days per week, one spent cold calling new prospects and the other spent generating proposals for our existing pipeline.

Personal Education Goal

- Poor Goal: I will learn more about my industry.
- SMART Goal: Over the next 12-months, I will read one industry-related article each weekday, actively engage in one industry-related LinkedIn group per week, present one topic-based presentation per quarter, and attend one industry conference within the year.

Health & Wellness Goal

- Poor Goal: I will improve my health.
- SMART Goal: I will lose 1.5 pounds per week, for a total of 15 pounds over 10 weeks. I will do so by a) taking two Pilates classes and participating in (3) 30-minute cardio sessions per week, b) following a 16/8 intermittent fasting schedule, c) tracking what I eat to prevent overeating, and d) checking in with Janet daily as my source of accountability.

Now that we have a solid understanding of SMART goals and how they look in practice, let's move on to the seventh and final component of a successful goal system.

#7 Reflect & Refine

Reflection and course correction are elemental to goal achievement. Consistently staying in touch with what's working, evaluating what's not, and adjusting where necessary dissipates roadblocks more quickly. Without intentionally allocating time to think and reflect, frustrations frequently resurface, and motivation begins to wane. However, when time is intentionally devoted toward thinking about, developing, and adjusting relevant strategies in the pursuit of goals, the power of those feedback loops begins to amplify positive outcomes.[18] This process works best when the included time slots occur daily, weekly, quarterly, and annually - a process we'll discuss in more detail in chapters nine and ten.

As Albert Einstein once famously said, "The world as we have created it is a process of our thinking. It cannot be changed without changing our thinking." It's often in the course of taking time to process our thoughts that we change our thinking, identify creative strategies for overcoming challenges, and find the path to achieving our goals - a process that strengthens the leader within, fuels success with science, and bridges the gap between planning and doing.

As an aside... **Big goals produce big results.** Circling back to the attainable aspect of SMART goals, just how big should your goals *really* be?

Famed author and leadership expert, Jim Collins, wrote about **BHAGs** (pronounced bee-hags) in his book *Built to Last*.[17]

BHAGs are big, hairy, audacious goals that push you beyond your comfort zone, force you to adopt a longer-term goal setting approach, and conceptually, are as easy to grasp as they are difficult to achieve. They mobilize your efforts, captivate your every thought, and become a guiding force in all other decision making.

The challenge with more simplistic goals is that they lack the intrinsic drivers to keep you motivated and engaged. The end result of such lackluster goals is often boredom and abandonment.

The best way to know if your meaningful goal is challenging enough is to do a gut check: *does it scare you?* If not, you may be playing it safe with goals that, simply put, are *too* easy.

The Art of Goal Setting

While the science of goal setting helps us understand the psychological principles that empower success, it's the art of goal setting that allows us to experiment with the process and find the solutions that best serve our individual strengths, style, and needs. Personalizing the goal getting experience to fit our individual nuances is often the difference between constructing a lifeless plan that sits on a shelf gathering dust and crafting one that invigorates the soul and propels energetic action on a daily basis.

The truth of this reality was highlighted for me when I was brought in to work with a sales team on their collective and individual efforts toward quota achievement. The newly promoted sales manager, Jon, had grown increasingly frustrated over his inability to generate consistent team results, a frustration that echoed loudly up the chain of command. In Jon's eyes, the answer was easy. If the team would simply follow the activity plan he had created for them - the very plan that had led to his personal success and promotion - consistent results would soon follow. However, it quickly became evident that his plan, while logical and orderly in its design, did not speak to the individual personalities that made up his team.

A mainstay of his plan required every sales rep to be in the office from 8 am - 11 am on Tuesdays and Thursdays to make a minimum of 50 customer outreach calls on each of those days. While the goal of making 100 phone calls per week had proven to be an effective strategy for producing consistent results, restricting how and when these calls took place was undermining the process. In all fairness, Jon thought his approach would bring an element of camaraderie to the group since everyone would be in the office working on the same goal at the same time. Noble in thought, but poor in execution. In practice, the approach resulted in group commiseration, which was eroding morale and diminishing respect for Jon as a leader.

Jon didn't understand the pushback from his team. From his perspective, he was genuinely trying to bolster their success, knowing that consistent activity would produce more sales and pad their pocketbooks. And who didn't want to increase their income? Unfortunately, what Jon failed to realize was that he wasn't giving them the flexibility or autonomy to achieve the 100-call per week goal in a fashion that fit who they were or made use of their natural strengths and talents. They weren't empowered; they were controlled.

Jon hadn't considered that his approach was more limiting than supportive, but with this new level of awareness, he wanted to find a better solution that worked for all. With a fresh perspective, a willingness to learn, and an eagerness to better support his team, we held a meeting to invite their feedback and input. The meeting was quite eye-opening for Jon. He learned that no one disagreed with the 100-call per week target - in fact, they all saw value in striving for this goal - it was simply the time and day mandates that were problematic. They also felt Jon didn't see them as individuals, treat them like adults, or give them the space to executive the target in a fashion that fit with their personalities.

As examples, a couple of reps shared that they felt more energized in the late afternoon and preferred to make their calls then. A few others voiced their strong preference for scheduling client meetings in the mornings, as fewer cancellations seemed to occur when they caught clients before the chaos of the day unfolded. Another rep shared that 50 calls a day left her tongue tied and exhausted; she preferred to break it up evenly over the week and make ten calls each day. What Jon soon came to realize was that, while his intentions were good, his structured format prevented his team from succeeding with the task.

By the end of the meeting, everyone felt heard and understood and a mutually beneficial solution was devised. Each team member committed to making 100 customer outreach calls each week and to sending Jon a brief outline detailing their plan for doing so. Jon agreed to support their individual approaches, knowing it was based on the strengths each rep brought to the table. Lastly, an equal agreement was made that Jon would only intervene if a rep missed their target. After a full month of testing this new approach, Jon was thrilled to see that the team had averaged 112 outreach calls per rep and that client meetings had increased by nearly 14% - a win-win that was celebrated by all.

Jon's experience demonstrates an important lesson. Meaningful goals that support larger initiatives are structurally important to the goal getting process. They speak to the *science* of goal setting and act as a catalyst toward incremental achievement. However, the nuanced means by which an individual takes goal-directed action is much more personalized and speaks to the *art* of goal setting. Balancing both the art and science of goal setting reminds us that success is not measured by the approach taken, but rather by the outcome produced by the actions themselves.

As we move into chapter nine, you'll craft a comprehensive goal plan that integrates the *science* of goal setting, but how you implement the action steps is where the *art* of goal setting takes center stage. Is there a time of day when your energy is most focused? Or a particular playlist that helps you get in the zone? Or a specific environment that energizes your thoughts and creativity? Now that you know how to develop habits and behaviors that are in alignment with your vivid vision and future self (chapter six), and how to experiment to find solutions that help you thrive (chapter seven), the next step is to craft your goal plan and infuse it with your personal style and flair.

chapter nine

Turning Vision into Reality

"The quality of our goals affects our motivation."

\- Marshall Goldsmith

Dane's Story cont.

In chapter one we met Dane, who led "a pretty decent life" by all accounts. Nothing was wrong, per se, but he couldn't shake the nagging sense that life was meant to be more than just "pretty decent". Motivated by his impending 50th birthday and feeling an intense need to dig deeper into his unrelenting restlessness, he put his faith in the STRENGTHENED framework and began his exploration.

When he completed the exercises included in chapter two and connected with the areas of interest that brought him the most joy, he realized his discontent stemmed from a deep-seated feeling that his work didn't bring enough meaning to his life. While it made profitable use of his MBA and enabled him to give his daughters the opportunities he never had growing up, it did nothing to brighten his heart or feed his soul.

As a child, there were many things Dane wanted to do but couldn't because his parents didn't have the means. He loved soccer, but the family couldn't afford the registration and uniform fees, so he was forced to watch from the sidelines instead of running up and down the field. He had great friends but wasn't allowed to attend their birthday parties because there was no money in the budget to buy gifts. Though Dane looks back on his childhood with a keen appreciation for how hard his parents worked to support the family, he equally remembers the sadness he felt as a kid and the burning desire he held to eventually create a different lifestyle for himself.

His high school grades and test scores had created a clear path to college, but even with three jobs, he couldn't escape the burden of college loans. Balancing a full course load with multiple jobs, Dane earned a bachelor's degree in finance before going on to complete his MBA. Driven to pay off his student loans as quickly as possible, he buried his head in his career, starting as an entry level data analyst and eventually climbing the corporate ladder into a senior financial analyst position with an ownership stake at a private equity firm. But as the years ticked on and the goal of paying off his debt was met, a meaningful direction in life felt elusive.

Dane's job, and the financial security it provided, was long in the making. His 14-year-old self, who despised the torn rags that lined his hand-me-down wardrobe, had set his sights on a career where tailored clothing and freshly shined shoes were the norm. Yet, achieving this milestone was no longer *enough*. He was incredibly grateful for his financial security and the opportunities it afforded him and his daughters, but he felt a pull to contribute to society in larger ways. As he reflected on the themes that surfaced during his exploration into his "Ideal Life", he realized his true passion lied in providing financial literacy education to at-risk and poverty-stricken teens. This was the one area where he truly lit up every time he participated in an event that served this need.

Once this awareness surfaced, it was like the dam had been broken. Suddenly, thoughts and ideas flooded his mind at every turn, bringing connections and opportunities into meticulous focus with extreme force. He channeled his insights into a clearly articulated vision, created a detailed goal plan in support of his vision, and got to work on bringing his vision to life.

As Dane learned, this process was far easier than he'd ever anticipated. By following a predictable, repeatable process (which is available to anyone willing to put in the work to design their purpose-driven future), complexity is replaced by clarity and a pathway to one's vision and goals concretely materializes.

From Vision to Reality

In the following pages, we're going to move through a seven-step process that will turn your vision for the future into a goal-oriented action plan for the present. The process essentially acts as a funnel, starting with the broader nature of your 5-year BHAGs and drawing them in tighter and tighter until arriving at your first action item in pursuit of your vision and goals. Visually, it looks like this:

While the process produces a singular and specific plan, it's not uncommon to create multiple goal plans for different areas of life. As examples, you may want to craft a career-oriented plan based on your professional goals, a financial plan that's guiding you toward early retirement, and a personal plan that enhances your intimate relationships. The good news is, once you've created your first plan, it's easy to duplicate the process and create goal plans specific to other areas of life.

The first step in beginning this process is to set aside an hour of disruption-free time to review everything you've captured in your downloadable workbook up until this point. This act will spark your PEA, stimulate your parasympathetic nervous system, and trigger your happy hormones, increasing your curiosity, interest, and openness to new ideas while promoting optimism. It's in this space that ideas surface and clarity evolves, so take your time and enjoy the process.

Once you've read through all your notes, turn to page 38 in your workbook and follow along with the seven-step process below.

Step 1: Use your vision statement to extrapolate and categorize your goals.

After revisiting your vision statement, use the space provided on page 38 of your workbook to create a list of the long-term goals that are embedded throughout. Don't overthink the process and don't limit yourself. Write every goal that surfaces for you, capturing those BHAGs (big hairy audacious goals) that are shining through the pages of your vision statement as well as all the smaller goals in between. You might find yourself writing down similar goals multiple times or identifying smaller goals that actually roll into bigger ones, but the objective here is to identify *all* your various goals and capture them in one place.

Once you've completed your comprehensive list, go back through with a fresh set of eyes, reading each goal and categorizing it according to the life area it addresses. Some category examples might include personal, professional, relationships and family, spiritual, financial, health and wellness, education. Once you've categorized each goal, take a step back and see what surfaces for you. Is there a particular area of life pulling at you more than others? Do you find that you have a longer list of goals in one area than all the others? Reflect on these insights before moving on.

Step 2: Determine which category and subsequent 5-year goal plan you'll begin with.

Looking at your list of goals and the respective categories applied to each, what is calling to you most deeply? Is there a category of goals that needs and deserves immediate attention? Is there a life area you've long neglected which will no longer take a back seat? Remember, challenging goals spur us to action and help drive motivation, so don't be tempted to take the easy road here. This is all about making your vision a reality, so ask yourself which category of goals are most important to bringing your vision to fruition.

Often the answer is quite obvious and leaps from the page. However, if you feel conflicted, remember that this is only the first goal plan. Once you learn the process, you can create multiple goal plans for each area of your life.

When you've made your decision, use the space on page 39 of your workbook to create a 5-year goal statement that incorporates the goals you've captured for that category. To help provide a framework for this step, here is the 5-year goal statement Dane created after connecting with the passions on his goal list:

"To create a national non-profit organization that provides mentorship, financial literacy education, and scholarship opportunities to disadvantaged, at-risk, poverty-stricken teens."

As you may notice, his 5-year goal statement is a bit broad and lacks some of the tenets of the SMART framework. However, that's perfectly acceptable and normal at this stage. Specificity and detail will be teased out once a deeper dive into the process occurs.

Step 3: Break your 5-year goal into five 1-year goals.

Now that you've established clarity surrounding your big picture, the next step is to break down your 5-year goal into five annual goals. These goals, when cumulatively achieved, will strategically lead to the overall accomplishment of your larger goal. In essence, you're creating a roadmap to get you from point A to point B. For some, starting with year five and working backwards is easier, but this step can be approached from either direction depending on which feels most logical to you.

In addition, just as road trips often take unplanned detours for the purpose of refueling, grabbing snacks, or visiting the world's largest ball of yarn, the journey between today and the achievement of your 5-year goal will have some detours of its own. For this reason, it's important to note that your timelines are not cast in stone and will shift as you begin traveling the goal-getters journey. Don't get paralyzed by this step expecting that you have to accurately predict the future, just craft the most logical incremental steps toward your 5-year goal as it stands today. Some goals will be achieved faster than projected, others will take longer than anticipated. The point in this exercise is to establish a basic framework, knowing that timeframes will inevitably and accordingly be adjusted when you "Reflect and Refine" on your progress along the way.

To see step 3 in action, let's look at Dane's annual goals:

Year 1: Draft the program and launch locally in beta.

Year 2: Finalize the program and roll out in surrounding counties.

Year 3: Transition from a local to a national presence, expanding into two neighboring states.

Year 4: Grow the formalized program and expand into five additional states, also further develop the online education portal with additional resources.

Year 5: Launch a "train the trainer" model and distribute the curriculum and resources across the country.

As you can see, Dane is starting to develop more specificity in his approach even though his annual goals are still a bit broad. This is perfectly fine as he's creating a framework to bring his vision to life - a framework that will naturally grow, change, and evolve as he begins to tighten his timeframe and dive into more detailed aspects of his plan.

Step 4: Break your first annual goal into 4-quarterly goals.

With your annual goals articulated, the next step is to break the year-1 goal into quarterly milestones. This is where the detail associated with your goals will start to flourish, bringing your vision-oriented plan into finer focus. As a reminder, you're essentially creating a goal-based roadmap where the cumulative achievement of each quarter's milestones leads to the completion of the annual goal, putting you 20% of the way toward your 5-year BHAG. Returning to Dane and keeping in mind that his year-1 goal was to "draft the program and launch locally in beta", here is how his quarterly goals unfolded:

Q1: Research the market and identify currently available programs. Evaluate the pros and cons of each program and make a list of what works and what doesn't. Enlist a core team to help me with the research process and provide insights and feedback. Assimilate the research notes into a basic outline to act as the rough framework for the program.

Q2: Draft version one and get the core team's feedback. Make adjustments as necessary. Begin creating assets.

Q3: Draft version two based on previous feedback and test with a small group locally. Tweak assets and support materials as needed.

Q4: Revise the program based on results from the local test group, create formalized program documentation, and launch first full course.

As you may have noticed, Dane's Q1 goal is far more detailed than the rest - a common occurrence that happens as a result of the close proximity of the 90-day goal. If you find yourself following a similar pattern, go with it. On the other hand, if you find yourself incorporating more detail across all quarters, that's beneficial as well. There is no right or wrong here. Both approaches will lead to success as a result of the upcoming steps in the process.

Step 5a: Break your first quarterly goal into 3-monthly goals.

Once you have clarity regarding the quarterly goals that will lead to the achievement of your first annual goal, the next step is to break the Q1 goal into 3-monthly goals. For Dane, the monthly goals he designed to propel him towards his Q1 objectives were as follows:

M1: Assemble a team to act as a review board and set up systems to capture and store research data.

M2: Divide research areas and define the types of details to be captured, including programs, target audience, marketing, technology, staff/volunteers, resources.

M3: Finalize and combine the research notes. Create a basic outline detailing various aspects to be potentially included in both the program and the business plan.

At this point, we have a rough framework for what the next 90-days should look like. This timeframe is the most critical in the process and is a powerful driver of success. It contains near-term goals that are purposely designed to support the achievement of your long-term BHAGs and does so in a way that promotes intrinsic motivation. This is the point where smaller action steps are constructed which, when stacked up over 90-days, leads to measurable results in the pursuit of your bigger vision. *This is one of the biggest keys to goal setting.*

When time frames are too far out, research has shown that motivation diminishes. Equally, when near-term goals aren't tied to a larger, more meaningful outcome, they slide into redundant, meaningless tasks that also decrease motivation. 90-days is the goal setting sweet spot because it's a long-enough time frame to make material progress, but short enough to course correct if things aren't headed in the intended direction. In addition, 90-day timeframes have been shown to fortify motivation while suppressing procrastination. For this reason, step 5 includes a second component.

Step 5b: Create a list of the action items that must be completed in order to achieve your monthly goals.

This is where fine details begin to really take shape. The goal here is to brainstorm as many action items as you can think of, while equally realizing that additional tasks will inevitably surface over time. Don't worry about the order, or which action items will fall in which week, just brainstorm and data dump every idea you think of, adding it to the appropriate months' list as you go.

As a point of clarification, it's important to delineate the difference between goals and tasks or action items:

- Goals are the end result, or objective, that you're seeking to achieve. These can be proximal or distal - in other words, short-, medium-, or long-term. An example of a goal is to contribute one original article per week to LinkedIn.

- Tasks and action items are essentially the to-dos that lead to the achievement of the goal and are always proximal (short term). Following from the previous example, article writing tasks may include choosing a subject matter, conducting research, writing the article, proofreading and formatting the piece, and posting to LinkedIn. Those are five individual tasks related to the one goal above.

An important tip for improved productivity and enhanced success: whenever possible and appropriate, create systems to support your goal getting efforts. Extending from the previous example, if one of your goals is to contribute 52 original articles to LinkedIn over the course of a year, then systemize this process so that is becomes predictable, repeatable, and *habitual*. This will empower you to make small adjustments to fine tune your approach instead of having to recreate the wheel every time. Remember, systems and routines line the path to freedom.

Once you've created comprehensive, action-oriented lists outlining the tasks that will lead to the achievement of your monthly goals, it's time to put these actions into practice.

Step 6: Break your first monthly goal into 4-weekly goals.

Returning to the monthly goals created in step 5a, the next step is to break your first monthly goal into four weekly goals. Like steps 3, 4 and 5a, these are sequential goals that stack upon one another leading to the achievement of the monthly goal. To see this in action, let's return to Dane's first monthly goal, which was to "Assemble a team to act as a review board and set up systems to capture and store research data." The weekly goals he outlined, which empowered him to systematically achieve his monthly goal, were as follows:

Week 1:

- Create a list of friends, family, and colleagues to enlist as support and/or as board members.
- Create a write up on each person so I'm clear on the value they bring and the role they could potentially play.
- Turn my vision statement into a 2-minute elevator pitch.

Week 2:

- Follow up with each individual to determine who's in and who's out.
- Make a list of their strengths and relevant experience.
- Find out the level of involvement they're willing to contribute. Are they open to monthly meetings?

Week 3:

- Host a zoom meeting so everyone can meet one another.
- Have everyone introduce themselves, share how they know me, and why they're willing to help with this adventure.
- Create and share a contact list so everyone has each other's info.

Week 4:

- Work with tech savvy team members to determine the best tools for capturing data.

- Create a how-to video or pdf walking people through the process of adding their research info to the system.
- Set up the selected tech tool and send each member documentation on how to use it.

A quick note of mention, not every month has four weeks but following this pattern sets you up for future success. Considering that each quarter is comprised of 13-weeks, consistently breaking monthly goals into four weekly subgoals leaves an extra week to play with at the end of each quarter. This can be essential if you're behind the eight ball and need a bit of extra time, and equally beneficial if you're ahead of the curve and want to knock a goal off the list for the following month. Once your weekly goals are established, it's time to begin the seventh and final step in this process.

Step 7: Break your weekly goals into daily tasks and to-dos.

Success is nothing more than a series of consistent action steps deliberately taken in the direction of your vision and dreams. If every single day, without fail, you do one thing in support of your goals, you'll find they quickly materialize right before your eyes. As you can see below, Dane's week one action items were quite specific and met all the tenets of the SMART goal structure, though none were excessively time consuming. His intention was to devote 60 - 90 minutes per day to this venture so as not to distract from his professional commitments. Here is how that process took shape for him.

Week 1:

Mon: Turn my vision statement into a 2-minute elevator pitch.

Tues: Present my elevator pitch to three trusted friends to get their feedback, then make adjustments based on their insights.

Wed: Create a list of friends, family, and colleagues who may potentially support me with this initiative.

Thurs: Write up a paragraph about each person on my list so I'm clear on my reasoning for calling them specifically.

Fri: Call the first half of the list. Explain why I'm calling and share my elevator pitch.

Sat: Make the remaining calls.

Sun: Create my action plan for next week.

Over the course of 18-months, Dane found this system allowed him to achieve his goals faster than he'd ever imagined. He was six months ahead of plan, had already rolled his program out in the surrounding counties, and was finalizing details for an impending launch in neighboring states. In addition, several members of his support team were well networked with contacts spanning across industries and state lines, which led to a bevy of sponsorships, donations, and volunteer support, all combining to help him breathe life into his vision.

Take Dane's story as a cautionary tale. If you follow this action-oriented, goal getting system, you may experience far quicker and bigger results than originally anticipated. You've been warned.

Building Your First Goal Plan

As a reminder, pages 38 - 44 of your workbook include the framework for you to design your initial goal plan, starting with your 5-year BHAG and drilling all the way down to your first action step. Once you've completed this process, the next (and perhaps, most important) step is to prioritize these actions in your daily calendar.

If your goal-oriented, vision-directed, carefully planned tasks don't get consistent priority in your daily schedule, then your efforts with this program were for not. Goal plans are only as effective as the action steps taken to support them. Without action, you have no progress. Without progress, your tomorrows will be no different than your yesterdays. However, if you follow the plan and take consistent action, your efforts will pay significant dividends.

In chapter eight, we reviewed the seven research-backed components of an optimal goal achievement system. Now that you've seen Dane's plan in action and are preparing to build your own, let's circle back to those components for a quick moment. As a reminder, they are:

- **Personally Meaningful** - (✓) This was achieved by crafting your vision and connecting with your values, then pulling your goals directly from the vision.

- **Goal Commitment** - (✓) This was inherently and intrinsically enhanced as a result of ensuring the goals were personally meaningful from the get-go.

- **Temporal Proximity** - (✓) Starting with your 5-year BHAG and drilling down to your first daily action ensured that a blend of short-, medium-, and long-term goals made up the structure of your goal plan.

- **SMART Goals** - (✓) As you look at Dane's goals above, you'll see that the systematic nature of this goal plan naturally leads to specific, measurable, achievable, relevant, and time-bound goals.

- **Daily Action** - (✓) Your goal plan gives you a roadmap for action, and the habits and behaviors you developed in chapters six and seven prepare you to take consistent action.

- **Accountability** - With your goal plan completed, evaluate the types of accountability you can layer into your system to enhance and ensure results.

- **Reflect & Refine** - Once your plan is in motion, set aside regular blocks of time to reflect on your results and refine your process. I highly recommend:

    o   15-minutes at the end of each day to review today's progress and make a solid plan for tomorrow;

    o   30-minutes at the end of each week to review and plan for the upcoming week; and

    o   Three hours at the end of each quarter to celebrate your successes, evaluate your challenges, and craft your next 90-day plan.

When one has a concrete, research-backed framework to build upon, and incorporates the individual style and flair that makes the plan work for them, their results soar. This is the art and science of goal setting. Follow this format and you'll be well on your way to making meaningful, measurable progress in the direction of your dreams.

chapter ten

The Path to Mastery

"People with high levels of personal mastery are continually expanding their ability to create the results in life they truly seek."

- Peter Senge

The Seeker's Journey

Congratulations! The steps you've taken to this point have set the stage for a bigger, bolder future. Your actions and efforts have declared that you're not willing to live life by default; you are among the rare few who have crafted a concrete plan to intentionally live life by design.

Does this mean everything will go perfectly according to plan? Absolutely not. Hurdles and setbacks will test your resolve, but you have a northern star to follow - a vivid vision that rests on a foundation of your core values and is made possible through the deliberate use of your signature strengths and supportive habits. You are on the path to achieving your big, hairy, audacious goals. You are on the path to mastery.

Beware though, personal mastery is not a one-time event achieved through the simple completion of a set of exercises within a book. It's an everlasting process that lives in perpetuity - a lifelong commitment to growth, reflection, learning, and development. Those seeking mastery know that reading a book or taking a class does not make one an expert.

Mastery unfolds over time as you incorporate the lessons learned and apply deliberate practice to the cycles of plateaus and progress that mark your journey. There are no quick fixes and no shortcuts. Mastery demands hard work, consistent action, and unwavering commitment. Patience and perseverance are required ingredients but, thankfully, they grow in spades as you expand your experience and knowledge, experiment with what you've learned, and intentionally employ your strengths to help you push beyond the boundaries of your comfort zone.

With dedication toward personal growth and an active interest in developing the leader within, you can step into the life you've dreamt and designed. As a reminder, the STRENGTHENED framework is simply one aspect, or subsystem, that fits within and complements your larger system. It gives you the tools and resources needed to create a personal success cycle of your own - one that empowers you to repeatedly reflect and refine as you make continual progress in the direction of your goals and dreams.

Personal Success Cycle

It's well established that success is a balanced blend of art and science. While this book and program were built on a research-backed, science-based framework, the real power of this system comes from how you choose to make it your own. Your journey to strengthen yourself and develop the leader within doesn't end here with chapter ten; it continues on through the personal success cycle you build for yourself and implement in your daily life.

The following pages outline tips and suggestions for building an empowering system that further enhances your growth and development. These are the strategies and techniques that, when layered on top of the STRENGTHENED framework, allow you to continue your path towards mastery.

As you read through the following components, consider how these strategies can be personalized to fit your current *and* future self while incorporating the signature strengths that are unique to you. When you build a system that's in intentional support of your vision and values, and purposefully plays to your strengths, personal mastery begins to unfold in new ways.

90-Day Plans: To revisit a conversation from chapter nine, 90-day goal plans that are in alignment with your long-term vision are one of the most powerful ways to make measurable progress toward your goals. This approach brings in the motivational drivers associated with temporal proximity while ensuring that consistency becomes a mainstay of your approach.

The 5-year goal plan you built is foundational to this process, so you're already well on your way, but if you'd like to take it a step further and amplify your results, I have a 90-day purpose-built planner that you can learn more about by visiting **http://lwm.link/planner**. Like STRENGTHENED, it's built on a research-backed, science-based framework and includes an e-coaching program to help you get the most out of your goal setting efforts.

Personal Meetings: How often do you schedule meetings with yourself? Yes, actually penciled into your agenda, blocked out in your digital calendar, and prioritized just as you would any other appointment. Scheduling regular meetings with yourself to reflect on your progress and refine your approach is essential to long-term success. It allows you to measure your results and adjust where necessary, while making space for new connections and insights to arise. How often should these meetings take place? I strongly advocate the following formula, which has been repeatedly proven to produce the strongest results.

- *Daily:* Set aside 10 - 15 minutes at the end of each day to review the current day's progress and create a concrete plan for the next. Planning for tomorrow after reviewing today ensures that your efforts and activities remain focused and deliberate. Success, after all, is nothing more than a series of consistent action steps taken one day after the next, and daily planning is a large part of that equation.

- *Weekly:* Schedule 30 - 45 minutes at the end of each week to reflect on the current week's progress and prepare for the week ahead. These weekly sessions allow you to take a closer look and determine whether any aspects of your plan need to be adjusted or refined. It's an opportunity to explore if you're on track with your timelines or if they need to be fine-tuned. It gives you the space to evaluate hurdles that may require additional help, support, or education and to establish a plan for overcoming them. Your weekly sessions are where you ensure that you're on track to meet the monthly goals you've set for yourself.

- *Monthly:* At the end of each month, set aside 60 - 90 minutes to review the progress you've made each week and evaluate how it contributed to the achievement of your monthly goals. Were you on target? Are there any adjustments that need to be made? Do you have a solid plan, including weekly goals and daily tasks, to support the upcoming month? Are you proactively working towards the life you've designed or reactively responding and living by default? Monthly meetings ensure that meaningful progress is being made in the direction of your larger vision and gives you an opportunity to recalibrate if you begin to veer off course.

- *Quarterly:* As previously noted, 90-day plans are essential to long-term success. They serve as the bridge between proximal and distal goals and bring us measurably closer to our vivid visions and future selves. They prevent time from slipping away and allow us to make material adjustments to our annual goals as needed. Those who follow this formula often delight in the fact that adjustments are frequently required because they're hitting their targets far faster than anticipated. When preparing for your personal quarterly meeting, block out 2 - 3 hours in your calendar, have your workbook and 5-year goal plan readily available, and reprint fresh copies of pages 41 - 44 from your workbook. With last quarter's plan in front of you, and fresh pages printed for the upcoming quarter, you're now prepared to continue your progress and craft a vision-specific goal plan for the upcoming quarter. (My 90-day agenda includes these planning pages as well. I promise this isn't a shameless plug. Well, maybe a little. But it truly is a supportive tool to further help you achieve your vision while developing the leader within.)

- *Annually*: This is my favorite meeting of the year. It's an opportunity to reflect on the past year's accomplishments, determine where you are in regard to your five-year plan, and set the goals and initiatives for the upcoming year. It's an opportunity to celebrate your successes, appreciate your growth, and revel in the progress you've made toward bringing your vision to life. While the length of this meeting is a matter of personal choice, it's important to give it the time and space it deserves. I have some clients who prefer long weekend getaways so they can unplug from their usual routine and immerse themselves in reviewing the previous year and planning for the next; others who prefer to do their planning as a brainstorming session with accountability partners; and others still who prefer to lock themselves in their offices for a day and focus on nothing but their goals for the upcoming year. Given that this meeting is about crafting meaningful, deliberate plans that will continue to advance your efforts and bring your vision to life, it's important to put yourself in an environment and setting that allows you to explore uninterrupted.

Annual Vision Tune-Ups: As progress is made and goals are achieved, it becomes increasingly important to revisit, update, and refine your vision. Often, advancements made in the direction of your dreams leads to natural enhancements in the details of your vision. Making these adjustments on an annual basis empowers you to craft deliberate goal plans that accelerate your path to achievement.

Combining your annual vision tune up with your yearly personal meeting is a phenomenal way to kickstart the new year and keep the momentum swiftly moving in your favor. It's also a great excuse for a mini vacation where you can unplug from the regular responsibilities of life and give yourself the creative space to craft your plans for the new year.

Daily Vision Visualization: A powerful method for staying connected to your vision is to read it daily, or better yet, record it as an audio file and listen to it every morning. As you read (or listen to) the vision, picture the details in your mind's eye. Doing so activates the PEA, anchors you to your future self, and serves as a reminder that visions are not about the details contained therein – they're about what a vision *does* to motivate, inspire, and perpetually propel you in the direction of your dreams.

Intentions: Do you ever have one of those mornings where your inner 5-year-old defiantly comes out and simply doesn't want to participate in what you have planned for the day? You know you need to get started on your tasks, but something inside of you is fighting it. You have clarity of purpose, goals that support your vision, and daily tasks that support those goals. So what's getting in the way?

Sometimes, despite our logical brains knowing what needs to be done, we just don't *feel* like it. In other words, our motivation has taken an impromptu mini-vacation and we need to get it reengaged. While the STRENGTHENED framework has psychological drivers embedded that naturally drive intrinsic motivation, there will still be days when your logical thoughts and emotional feelings are misaligned. When this happens, it can help to apply the following formula: $A^{(T+F)} = GA$.

> Action, when amplified by the power of thoughts *and* feelings, leads to goal achievement.

But how do you engage your feelings when they're burrowed under the bedsheets and refusing to start the day? While there are a variety of ways to achieve this, many of which are strewn throughout this program, there is one simple yet powerful technique we have yet to explore, and that's the power of intention.

When you set a deliberate intention and spend a few minutes focusing on it, research has shown that the prefrontal cortex is activated, setting off a chain reaction where the executive function in your brain is mobilized to get your thoughts and feelings in alignment.[1]

The next time you feel your motivation going on holiday, grab a pen and a piece of paper and physically write out your intention for the day. This is not about writing a goal or task, but a true intention that taps into the positive networks of your brain. Once it's on paper, spend a minute or two reflecting on what you just wrote so that your brain can process your feelings and emotions at a deeper level. Let me share a personal example to put this in context.

In this course of writing this book, I hit a wall half-way through where my inner child wanted to go out and play - every. single. day. - instead of focusing on the writing goals that were deliberately designed to support my bigger vision. I realized my thoughts and feelings were at odds with one another, so I began starting each day with a purposeful intention. Here is one of the intentions I captured in my agenda:

> "Today the words will flow from me with ease. I'll have fun capturing the insights that already exist in my knowledge base and will enjoy the process of giving words to my thoughts. At the end of the day, I'll be

proud and inspired by what I wrote knowing it serves my larger purpose of helping others to develop the leader within."

As you can see, the intention is about the *feelings* I'll experience in the process of completing my tasks for the day. Those tasks support my larger goals, and those goals are in alignment with my vision and purpose. When intentions become the deliberate focus, outcomes follow in short order. $A^{(T+F)} = GA$

Accountability: Do you remember what Dr. Gail Matthews' research revealed? (We explored her insights in chapter eight.) Individuals whose systems included an accountability partner experienced double the goal getting success rate of those who didn't.[2] Her research brilliantly demonstrated the influential impact that accountability has on motivation, performance, and achievement.

When you commit to a deadline for when you'll share progress updates with another person, it serves as a forcing function that motivates effort and keeps your momentum in full swing. After all, who wants to tell their accountability partner, "I took zero action toward the goals I set for myself today". Additionally, accountability partners can be a wonderful sounding board for when you're stuck or can't see the forest for the trees.

For this reason, it's important to partner with someone whom you trust enough to be completely honest and vulnerable with, but who also has the relevant background and experience to provide valuable insights. Just remember, you're partners thus the relationship is a two-way street. While it can admittedly take a bit of effort to find the right fit, a mutually beneficial accountability partnership is worth its weight in gold and will pay huge dividends toward bringing each of your respective visions to life.

One-on-one partnerships, however, are not the only form of accountability. In fact, they're simply one aspect of partner-based accountability. Additional options include hiring a coach, finding a mentor, and joining a mastermind group, all of which are equally powerful ways of holding yourself accountable through the relationships you form with others.

Alongside partner-based accountability is also the importance of embedding self-accountability into your personal success system. This can include activities such as using a daily agenda to intentionally plan your work and work your plan, reviewing your efforts daily and seeking incremental improvement (see "Did I Do My Best?" below), holding regular meetings with yourself to reflect and refine (see "Personal Meetings" above), and utilizing a habit tracker to track your performance.

When you find the right combination of accountability methods to layer into your personal success cycle, your vision-directed efforts will be amplified in immeasurable and meaningful ways.

Did I Do My Best?: Let's be honest, sometimes unexpected stuff gets in our way, derailing our efforts and preventing us from achieving our daily goals. That said, it's still up to us to decide if choice, not circumstance, will determine our future. Each day is a fresh opportunity to start anew. A chance to be present and focused on that *one* day, recognizing that each morning begins with a fork in the road. Will you choose the goal-directed path that's in alignment with your vision and values, or the reactive path that leaves your future up to chance? Admittedly, it can sometimes be difficult in the moment to identify which path you're on but conducting a daily assessment of your efforts is one of the most surefire ways to get you back on track when things start to go awry.

While there are several ways to approach this task and recalibrate your efforts, the most powerful technique I've witnessed comes from Marshall Goldsmith, best-selling author and renowned leadership coach.[3] His simple process brings each day to a close with a series of questions that begins with "Did I do my best to...?". The six foundational questions he recommends are:

- Did I do my best to set clear goals today?
- Did I do my best to make progress on my goals today?
- Did I do my best to find meaning and purpose today?
- Did I do my best to be happy today?
- Did I do my best to build positive relationships today?
- Did I do my best to be fully engaged today?

As you can see, these questions bring inquiry and reflection to life while requiring personal ownership in the process. The questions don't ask if your partner made you happy today, or if others in the workplace were fully engaged today, but rather, puts the onus for a happy, productive, and intentional life squarely on your shoulders.

While these six questions are incredibly effective, the real power in this approach comes from creating additional customized questions that are specific to you, your vision and goals, and the values you strive to live into every day. For me, some of my personal questions include:

- Did I do my best to prioritize distraction-free time with my husband today?
- Did I do my best to contribute value to my leadership communities today?
- Did I do my best to communicate gratitude and appreciation to my clients today?

The questions will be different for everyone, but the act of designing them in direct support of your future self and bigger vision is a powerful means of keeping yourself continually moving in the direction of your dreams.

Now, when a bad day hits and you find your original plans drifting off course, you can quickly assess your response, *which is the only thing you have control over*, and reset your intentions for the next day.

As a quick reminder, all of these processes are about experimenting with yourself to craft customized solutions that help you thrive. While Goldsmith recommends the questions as an evening exercise, I have several clients who found it more empowering to answer them first thing in the morning. Essentially, they begin each day evaluating if they did their best the day before, which keeps them on track while spurring their efforts and energies in the current day. Play with the questions and timing until you unlock a combination that empowers you to flourish. This is the art of being STRENGTHENED and developing the leader within.

Unplug, Play, Rest, and Reset (UPRR): As important as it is to take consistent action in the direction of your goals and dreams, it's equally important to intentionally carve out time and space to unplug, play, rest, and reset. Without regular opportunities for neurological rejuvenation, our cognitive resources become depleted, creativity diminishes, and problem-solving abilities decline. Not to mention the general crankiness that accompanies an "all work, no play" approach - or maybe that's just me.

While it's frequently acknowledged that humans need an average of 7-hours of sleep each night in order to thrive and flourish, the important role of play is often overlooked. As Stuart Brown, M.D. wrote in *Play: How it Shapes the Brain, Opens the Imagination, and Invigorates the Soul*, "[play] energizes us and enlivens us. It eases our burdens. It renews our natural sense of optimism and opens us up to new possibilities".[4] As his research has shown, play is a catalyst to creativity that increases productivity while favorably impacting positive emotion and engagement, two important elements of PERMA.[5]

The UPRR equation is different for everyone and requires personal experimentation, but finding the right mix is an important exercise. Some examples which others have included in their ideal UPRR mix include:

- Creating evening routines that set the stage for a solid night's sleep.
- Finding dedicated times during the day to meditate or think.
- Having a regular exercise schedule, even if it consists of nothing more than routine walks.
- Taking time out to color or do puzzles.
- Scheduling a "play date" each week with a friend or loved one.
- Setting time aside each day to curl up with a good book.
- Planning weekend getaways on a quarterly basis for a deeper opportunity to unplug and reset.

Though it may seem counterintuitive, sometimes the best way to make considerable progress toward your vision and goals is by taking a step back and giving yourself a little break. When you remove yourself from the tasks and challenges at hand, and do so on a consistent basis, it makes space for your subconscious to go to work in the background and for your neural networks to bring fresh perspectives and new solutions to the surface.

Making It Your Own

Your personal success cycle is just that... *yours* and *personal*. While the list above is nowhere close to exhaustive, it does provide some cornerstone behaviors to consider when crafting a plan that will support your ongoing growth and development. Just remember to keep experimenting, reflecting, and refining. Without consistent action and a perpetual dedication toward growth and learning, the vision and goals we hold for our future can quietly fade away into oblivion, leaving all our tomorrows the same as our yesterdays.

⇒ **Exercise #1**: Visit page 45 in your workbook and craft a personal success cycle to carry you beyond the pages of this book. Consider which aspects you'll incorporate from the list above and how frequently each act will take place. Be as specific as possible knowing that ongoing success lives in the small details that add up to big changes.

If We Were Face-to-Face

If you and I we're working one-on-one, I'd be high-fiving you right now for the tremendous efforts you've poured in to developing the leader within. 🖐 What you've done is no easy feat! You've embodied Jerry Rice's famous mantra, "Today I will do what others won't, so tomorrow I can accomplish what others can't." You've put yourself on the path to a bolder future.

As we part ways, there are a few pieces of advice which I consistently share with clients and would like to share with you as well. These aren't new or novel thoughts, and many of them fall under the category of common sense, but they're important nuggets to remember and continually apply.

Live life by design, not by default. Far too many people live reactively, responding to whatever life throws at them and failing to chart their own course. You, clearly, are not one of those people. You are STRENGTHENED and understand the immense value embedded in the process of developing the leader within. If you wanted an average life, you wouldn't have picked up this book, so continue your journey with gusto and zest. Develop a personal success cycle that steadily propels you to be your best self and be sure to celebrate all your marvelous victories, both big and small, along the way.

Setting, pursuing and achieving goals are acts of leadership. When someone has clarity surrounding their values-based vision for the future, develops a goals-based strategy to implement the vision, and takes daily action in support of those goals, they have the power to change the world. Your vision and purpose surfaced for a personally meaningful reason and your unique way of bringing your gifts to the world is critically important. Don't stop living into your future self and don't stop taking daily goal-directed action. Some days will be fun and energizing, others will be difficult and draining, but keep your eye on the bigger picture and your vision for the future will soon become your present reality.

Model the way. How you show up sets the stage for those around you. Demonstrating your commitment to your values and purpose will naturally challenge others to do the same. Leading by example creates a breadcrumb trail for others to follow. True, some acts of leadership are obvious and external, but often it's the intrinsic nature of how one shows up and shines that separates good leaders from great ones.

As a culminating act of inquiry and reflection, I have three final exercises for you to complete:

⇒ **Exercise #2**: Retake the PERMA assessment and compare your original scores with your current scores. Page 46 of your workbook includes space for you to do so, as well as room to detail any insights or thoughts that arise in the process.

⇒ **Exercise #3**: Retake the 12-point questionnaire that originally appeared in chapter one. Space to do so has been provided on page 47 of your workbook. Compare the pre- and post-results and capture any thoughts or ideas about these changes in the included notes area.

⇒ **Exercise #4**: With the above exercises completed, move to page 48 in your workbook and spend a few minutes reflecting on the work you've done in this program. What have you learned? How have you grown or changed? What lessons will you take with you going forward?

Remember, you're not the same person you were when you started this book and program. You've evolved in the direction of your future self and will continue to do so with each intentional day. My wish for you is to live life boldly, shine bright at every opportunity, and enjoy the journey as you continue to step into your vision and develop the leader within.

10 Principles for Leaders to Live By

1. Prime your neural networks by fueling your success with science.
2. Anchor yourself daily to the motivational power of your vision.
3. Let your values and purpose guide your everyday actions and efforts.
4. Leverage your unique combination of strengths to amplify your results.
5. Practice daily habits that are in alignment with your future self.
6. Set yourself up for daily success by intentionally owning every morning.
7. Keep your goals front and center, making continual progress in the direction of your dreams.
8. Build mutually beneficial, accountability-enhancing relationships.
9. Take time to rejuvenate by unplugging, playing, resting, and resetting.
10. Never stop experimenting, learning, and developing the leader within.

Appendix A: The Six Virtues and Their Respective Strengths

The information that follows draws from the extensive body of research published in *Character Strengths and Virtues: A Handbook and Classification*.[1] A basic overview of each virtue is provided, as well as the associated character strengths.

Wisdom: The virtue of Wisdom consists of cognitive strengths that involve the acquisition of knowledge and experience which is then used for good. These strengths include Creativity, Curiosity, Judgment, Love of Learning, and Perspective. Use of the cognitive strengths leads to a practical intelligence that balances the interests of the self, others, and community as a whole.

- **Creativity** (originality, ingenuity): Thinking of new and unique ways to do things. Conceptualizing novel, uncommon or different approaches. Creativity can include and incorporate artistic achievement but is not limited to it.

- **Curiosity** (interest, novelty-seeking, openness to experience): Taking an interest in subjects, topics and experiences for their own sake and not (necessarily) as a means to an end. Finding areas of interest to be fascinating and worthy of further exploration.

- **Judgment** (critical thinking, open-mindedness, rationality): Examining scenarios from every angle, weighing evidence fairly and justly, and reflecting on information thoroughly to avoid rushing to conclusions. Being able to adjust one's position or change one's mind in light of presenting evidence.

- **Love of Learning**: Systematically building one's skillsets and/or adding to their body of knowledge to master particular topics or subjects. This can be done informally, as a personal endeavor, or through formal education. This is related to Curiosity but moves beyond mere interest in a subject, allowing for new knowledge to be acquired and leveraged.

- **Perspective** (integrating viewpoints): Being able to look at the bigger picture, consider other points of view, and offer sage advice and wise counsel to others. The ability to look at situations in ways that help make sense for oneself and others.

Courage: The virtue of Courage consists of emotional strengths that involve overcoming challenges, both internal and external, to achieve one's desired goals. These strengths include Bravery, Perseverance, Honesty, and Zest. Use of the emotional strengths promotes pushing through challenges, living in alignment with values, and acting on convictions and beliefs even when doing so is difficult.

- **Bravery** (valor): Taking action in the face of fear, difficulty, challenge, or pain. Doing what needs to be done, speaking up for what is right, and acting on convictions, even when doing so is the unpopular choice or threats are perceived.

- **Perseverance** (industry, persistence): Pushing persistently through obstacles to finish what one starts. Taking pleasure in the completion of tasks and the achievement of goals.

- **Honesty** (authenticity, integrity): Being true to oneself, both publicly and privately, and presenting oneself authentically and genuinely. Being truthful in thought and speech while taking responsibility for one's own actions and emotions.

- **Zest** (vitality, vigor, energy): Living life to the fullest with exuberance, excitement and energy. Approaching life as an adventure to be lived whole-heartedly and with a sense of vitality and aliveness.

Humanity: The virtue of Humanity consists of interpersonal strengths that focus on building and cultivating relationships. These strengths include Love, Kindness, and Social Intelligence. Use of the interpersonal strengths promotes deeper understandings of human nature, a desire to guard and protect relationships, and showing kindness and generosity without expectation.

- **Love** (loving others, being loved by others): Valuing close, connected relationships with others. This can include love for those who care for you, love for those whom you care for, and reciprocal relationships where love and care are mutually shared.

- **Kindness** (generosity, nurturance, care, compassion, altruism, niceness): Performing good deeds, doing favors, and helping others without reciprocal expectations.

- **Social Intelligence** (emotional intelligence, personal intelligence): Knowing how to adapt and fit into different social situations while possessing insights and awareness into the motives and feelings of others and oneself. Understanding what motivates people and makes them tick.

Justice: The virtue of Justice consists of civic strengths that seek to bolster equity and improve community health. These strengths include Teamwork, Fairness, and Leadership. Use of civic strengths promote stronger interactions within communities and among people, while building towards fairness and equality.

- **Teamwork** (citizenship, social responsibility, loyalty): Being a loyal member of a group or team who pulls one's own weight and does their fair share to support group initiatives. Prioritizes efforts for the good of the group over personal gain.

- **Fairness** (care-based, justice-based, moral reasoning): Applying notions of fairness and justice to mitigate biased thoughts and decisions about others. Treating people equally, giving everyone fair chances and equitable opportunities.

- **Leadership**: Influencing, inspiring and encouraging a group of individuals to achieve common tasks and goals while maintaining positive, productive relations within the group.

Temperance: The virtue of Temperance consists of strengths that foster moderation while protecting against excess. These strengths include Forgiveness, Humility, Prudence, and Self-Regulation. Use of these strengths promote self-restraint, leading to a reduction in the types of negative behaviors that often prompt an array of personal and social problems.

- **Forgiveness**: Accepting the wrong-doings and shortcomings of others, giving people second chances, and letting bygones be bygones.
- **Humility** (modesty): Holding an accurate, uninflated view of oneself and keeping one's accomplishments and achievements in perspective, allowing them to speak for themselves.
- **Prudence**: Being mindful of one's choices and the implications they hold for the future. Being careful not to say or do things that may later be regretted.
- **Self-Regulation** (self-control): Showing control over one's thoughts, impulses, emotions, and actions. Demonstrating discipline in the pursuit of goals.

Transcendence: The virtue of Transcendence consists of strengths that connect us to a meaning or purpose that is larger than ourselves. These strengths include Appreciation of Beauty and Excellence, Gratitude, Hope, Humor, and Spirituality. Use of these strengths promote a deeper, more meaningful connection to the universe.

- **Appreciation of Beauty and Excellence** (awe, wonder, elevation, admiration): Noticing beauty and excellence across multiple domains of life, such as art, nature, science, selfless deeds of others, and everyday experiences. Emotionally experiencing the awe and wonder of beauty and excellence and appreciating it profoundly.

- **Gratitude**: An awareness of the treasured moments, gifts, and opportunities that come one's way and sensing and expressing sincere thankfulness in response.

- **Hope** (optimism, future mindedness, future orientation): Holding an optimistic view for a positive future, believing it can be brought about, and acting in ways that facilitate the desired outcome of that future.

- **Humor** (playfulness): Seeing the lighter side of life, bringing smiles to others, infusing situations with laughter, and injecting playfulness and good cheer to produce positive emotions in oneself and others.

- **Spirituality** (purpose, meaning, faith, religiousness): Holding coherent beliefs about the higher purpose of the universe, the meaning of life, and one's place within both. Having personal practices and beliefs surrounding the universe or a higher power that shapes one's conduct while providing comfort.

Appendix B: The 24-Character Strengths

The information that follows draws from the extensive body of research on character strengths and virtues[2] and is designed to provide actionable insights on how to leverage your unique combination of strengths.

Each strength has an in-depth overview that includes:

- A quote that embodies the strength.
- A definition of the strength, as drawn from *Character Strengths and Virtues: A Handbook and Classification*.[3]
- Examples of the strength in action, both in simple and more complex terms.
- An explanation of the continuum of use, providing insights on how a strength looks when under, over, or optimally used.
- Three exercises to help you build that specific strength.
- A recommended film that demonstrates the strength in action. Each film description includes enough detail so you know what to look for, but not so much that it spoils the film or eliminates your ability to engage in strengths-spotting.
- Inquiry questions for you to introspect and reflect on.
- A summary point that defines the strength's core essence.

Strength: **Appreciation of Beauty and Excellence** (awe, wonder, elevation, admiration) | Virtue: Transcendence

"Appreciation is a beautiful thing: It makes what is excellent in others belong to us as well." - Voltaire

Definition: Noticing beauty and excellence across multiple domains of life, such as art, nature, science, selfless deeds of others, and everyday experiences. Emotionally experiencing the awe and wonder of beauty and excellence and appreciating it profoundly.

Strength in Action:
- *Simple Application:* Marveling at the incredible array of colors gracing the sky during a peaceful morning sunrise.
- *Complex Application:* Taking notes during a colleague's presentation to acknowledge and admire the various ways they excelled in their communication, delivery, and connection with the audience.

Continuum of Use:
- *Underuse:* Being mindless and oblivious to the everyday beauty and excellence that exists.
- *Optimal Use:* Having an appreciation for the variety of ways and the range of areas where beauty and excellence can be found.
- *Overuse:* Excessively applying or expecting a level of beauty and excellence that speaks to snobbery and perfection.

3 Actions to Build Appreciation of Beauty and Excellence:
- Grab a notebook and spend a day taking note of the beauty and excellence that exists all around you and the different formats it presents itself in. As examples, this might include the beauty of a sunrise that greets you in the morn, the excellent performance of a

colleague who consistently wows others with the calibration of their presentation skills, or the admiration you hold for a friend who overcomes major life challenges with grace and compassion. At the end of the day, read the notes you took and spend a few minutes focusing on the awe and wonder that was beautifully woven throughout your day.

- Think of three people whom you interacted with today and identify one or two character strengths each individual displayed during your exchange. Take note of how those character strengths contribute to who that person is, then spend a few minutes appreciating the ways their character strengths positively contribute to those around them.

- Set the stage for a day of awe and wonder. Choose an activity that immerses you in a style of beauty and excellence that you naturally connect with, then take a notebook with you as you head out on your adventure. Take notes each time you find yourself in awe throughout the day, detailing what captivated your thoughts and emotions and why it was so moving. Revisit the notes whenever you need an energizing reminder of the beauty and excellence that fuels your soul.

Recommended Film: *Elf.* Buddy, who grew up at the North Pole believing he was an elf, has his heart broken when he overhears the other elves saying he's actually a human and that's why he lacks proficient toy making skills. Not wanting to believe these vicious rumors, Buddy approaches Santa only to find out he is indeed human, and worse yet, his biological father is on Santa's naughty list. Buddy travels to New York with hopes of redeeming his father's naughty status, and while nothing goes according to plan, what ensues are myriad adventures filled with amazement and delight as he marvels at every new experience.

From the delectable taste of syrup (which he puts on everything, including his spaghetti) to the joy of working in a mailroom (which most others find depressing), Buddy exemplifies *appreciation of beauty and excellence,* demonstrating the awe and wonder that can be found in even the most mundane of experiences. Throughout the film, his deep sense of *curiosity* leads him to an abundance of opportunities and experiences, which he regularly expresses *gratitude* and thankfulness for. This funny, uplifting film provides countless examples of appreciation of beauty and excellence commingling with its two highest correlates, gratitude and curiosity.

Inquiry and Reflection:

- Looking back on yesterday, what simplicities presented themselves and filled you with a sense of appreciation? What are some everyday examples of excellence that you commonly happen upon or witness? What are some examples of people, things, or events that you used to marvel at, but now take for granted because of the frequency with which they occur? What steps can you take to slow down and find excellence in everyday experiences?

- Thinking back on the last week, do you more frequently appreciate and admire things of beauty or examples of excellence? Why do you suppose you lean more towards one over the other? What steps can you take to elevate your appreciation of both beauty and excellence in a balanced way?

- Excellence is often showcased in the moral goodness of others. Thinking back over the last week, what acts of moral goodness did you witness? What response did you have upon recognizing such behavior? Did you express your appreciation outwardly or was it an internal feeling? What lessons can you take from the various acts you saw and how they made you feel?

Core Essence: Profound appreciation. Seeing beyond the surface to experience awe and wonder.

Strength: **Bravery** (valor) | Virtue: Courage

"Believe in yourself. You are braver than you think, more talented than you know, and capable of more than you imagine." - Roy T. Bennett

Definition: Taking action in the face of fear, difficulty, challenge, or pain. Doing what needs to be done, speaking up for what is right, and acting on convictions, even when doing so is the unpopular choice.

Strength in Action:

- *Simple Application:* Having a tough but necessary conversation with someone.
- *Complex Application:* Pushing through the fear of public speaking to deliver a meaningful speech in support of an important social initiative.

Continuum of Use:

- *Underuse:* Allowing excessive fear to provoke cowardice and prevent action-taking.
- *Optimal Use:* Confronting adversity and taking action in the face of physical, moral, or psychological fear.
- *Overuse:* Disregarding or failing to acknowledge legitimate concerns or behaving in a reckless, foolhardy manner.

3 Actions to Build Bravery:

- Make a list of 10 things you're fearful of, then choose an item to take action on. Some examples might include taking a swim lesson if you're fearful of water, joining Toastmasters if you fear public speaking, or taking a communications course to overcome a fear of confrontation.
- Engage in mental rehearsal and visualization before embarking on an anxiety-provoking situation. Picture yourself being brave as you walk

through the scenario in your mind and envision how your courage will positively impact the outcome.

- Spend a day intentionally looking for common examples of brave, courageous acts. Examples can be found in the way a coworker speaks up for another colleague, a child who hesitantly climbs on a bicycle for the first time, a news story about firefighters rushing into a burning building to save others, or the simple act of bravely being honest with a friend. Journal the insights and a-ha's that arise as a result.

Recommended Film: *Raiders of the Lost Ark*. As Indiana Jones' character repeatedly illustrates, brave people aren't free from fear, they're simply willing to face their fears and push through them. An example of Jones' balanced and optimal use of bravery can be seen in his paralyzing fear of snakes, which manifests as both a physical and psychological fear. When his anxieties are provoked by a pit of snakes that stand between him and his goal, he doesn't cower or freeze in the face of threat nor does he recklessly storm the snake-filled pit. Instead, he acknowledges his fear, takes a moment to evaluate the situation, and then takes the necessary action to continue moving forward.

Jones also demonstrates moral *bravery* in his willingness to do (and teach) what's right even when it's not the popular opinion. His role as a professor highlights his uncanny ability to make sense of the various patterns that exist in the chaos, showcasing the *perspective* he brings to the equation. Additionally, his knack for understanding different social and cultural norms and blending into their environments is indicative of his *social intelligence*. Bravery is most highly correlated with Perspective and Social Intelligence and Jones provides a wonderful example of how the combination of these strengths can produce meaningful results.

Inquiry and Reflection:

- Bravery can be found in acts that challenge physical fears (such as Indiana Jones' fear of snakes), moral fears (like standing up for your convictions despite potential ridicule), or psychological fears (such as pushing through anxieties associated with public speaking). Reflecting on these categories, think of a fear you recently encountered but were able to push through. What gave you the strength to overcome the fear? Do you find any of these categories more challenging than others? Why or why not?

- Saying yes is often easier than saying no - confrontation is avoided and no justification is required when you agree to someone's request. However, people frequently feel obligated to justify their reasoning when declining an invitation or request. Reflecting back on a recent situation when you agreed to something but regretted doing so, what influenced your decision in the moment? Which end of the continuum of use was your bravery operating from? How will you leverage your bravery to produce a different outcome in the future?

- Courage and bravery can be mustered in both large and small ways. Reflect on a small yet brave action from today, such as a phone call you feared making or necessary feedback you delivered to a colleague. How did you feel leading up to the act? What empowered you to push through the fear and follow through? How did you feel afterwards? Is there anything you would do differently if you had the opportunity to address it again?

Core Essence: Tackling adversity. Acknowledging fear but not allowing it to limit action.

Strength: **Creativity** (originality, ingenuity) | Virtue: Wisdom

"Creativity is intelligence having fun." - Unknown

Definition: Thinking of new and unique ways to do things. Conceptualizing novel, uncommon, or different approaches. Creativity can include and incorporate artistic achievement but is not limited to it.

Strength in Action:
- *Simple Application:* Making up a silly rhyme to entertain a child.
- *Complex Application:* Using kitchen tongs in an out-of-the-box way to hold papers in place and prevent them from blowing off an easel while conducting an outdoor workshop.

Continuum of Use:
- *Underuse*: Conforming to standard approaches; following prescribed solutions.
- *Optimal Use*: Generating adaptive, original ideas; contributing unique solutions.
- *Overuse*: Demonstrating eccentric behaviors that are less likely to be embraced.

3 Actions to Build Creativity:
- Think of a challenge you're currently facing and brainstorm a list of ten different and unlikely solutions. They don't necessarily need to be serious or viable contenders; they just need to be "out of the box" solutions that are approached in a novel and unique way.
- Grab an everyday object, reflect on its intended use, then make a list of ten creative, alternative ways the object could be used.
- Get a blank piece of paper and a pen or pencil, then draw a picture or write a poem reflecting a happy memory from the day before. Art skills

and poetic prowess are not required, this is simply a creative exercise for the brain.

Recommended Film: *Disney's Beauty and the Beast.* Maurice, Belle's father, is initially depicted as an eccentric inventor, demonstrating how he frequently overuses his creativity in unusual ways. However, he positively leverages this character strength to generate an adaptive and original idea - a unique machine for chopping wood. As the story progresses, he demonstrates further creativity by using his invention in a novel way to solve a more pressing problem and save his daughter's life.

In addition to his strength of creativity, Maurice also displays an on-going *curiosity* for the things around him, a signature strength equally shared by his daughter, as well as *bravery* and courage, which are front and center when he ventures back to the castle on his own to rescue Belle from the Beast. Curiosity and bravery are the highest correlated strengths with creativity, and this film demonstrates how the strengths support each other in character development and problem solving.

Inquiry and Reflection:

- In what areas of life does your creativity regularly surface? How do your creative approaches support and benefit you?
- Consider a recent challenge. Did your creativity play a role in crafting a solution? Looking back, how could you heighten creativity in addressing that particular challenge?
- When is your creativity at its best? Does it flourish in certain situations, conditions, or environments? When is it most restricted? Are there certain situations, conditions, or environments that reduce it?

Core Essence: Practical uniqueness. Seeing and doing things in surprising or unique ways that are outside the norm.

Strength: **Curiosity** (interest, novelty-seeking, openness to experience) | Virtue: Wisdom

"We keep moving forward, opening up new doors and doing new things, because we're curious… and curiosity keeps leading us down new paths."
- Walt Disney

Definition: Taking an interest in subjects, topics and experiences for their own sake and not (necessarily) as a means to an end. Finding areas of interest to be fascinating and worthy of further exploration.

Strength in Action:

- *Simple Application:* Asking a colleague a question or two about themselves.
- *Complex Application:* Letting your love of ice cream take you on an explorative journey into the flavor profiles of various fruits and spices and then experimenting with your own ice cream flavors at home.

Continuum of Use:

- *Underuse:* Demonstrating disinterest and apathy that can equally appear as boredom.
- *Optimal Use:* Taking a genuine interest in exploration and novel experiences.
- *Overuse:* Appearing nosy and prying in a potentially intrusive and meddlesome way.

3 Actions to Build Curiosity:

- Choose an area of interest or intrigue and then spend 30-minutes each day for a week exploring the topic further through videos, articles, and books. Keep notes on any exciting or intriguing insights you discover, then revisit and reflect on your notes at the end of the week.

- Choose a culture or country you've wanted to learn more about, then spend 30-days immersing yourself in various aspects of their culture. You can explore travel shows that teach you more about the area, experiment with local recipes, watch movies set and filmed in that country, read books that explore their history, and learn common phrases in their language, as examples.

- Take an online course in a subject you've repeatedly found yourself curious about. The options available online are wide and varied, teaching everything from film making to writing to language to dancing to cooking, and everything in between.

Recommended Film: *Disney's Alice in Wonderland.* Alice's perpetual curiosity leads her on a variety of exciting adventures, which she repeatedly greets with openness and intrigue. While admittedly, her curiosity is sometimes overused and shows up as nosiness (such as when she *must* know who the White Rabbit is and what he's up to), it's equally rewarding for her. Chasing her curiosity with zeal and gusto leads to novel experiences, exciting explorations, and new insights that would not have surfaced if it weren't for her unending curiosity-driven pursuits.

Throughout her adventures, she also regularly employs *creativity* to look at her unusual surroundings with a fresh perspective and to craft adaptive, unique solutions for the complex challenges that arise in this environment. In addition, she approaches her adventures with a sense of energy, exuberance, and excitement, demonstrating the *zest* she has for life. Curiosity and zest (along with love of learning) are the highest correlated strengths associated with curiosity, and Alice's character illustrates these beautifully.

Inquiry and Reflection:

- Think about the last subject or topic you explored. Why did you choose this particular subject and what insights did you gain in the process? How did the explorative endeavor make you feel?

- Curiosity is often used at varying levels in different areas of life. Where do you find your curiosity thrives most? Where is it most constrained?

- Reflect on a time when your curiosity toward one subject led to meaningful insights in another area (i.e., watching a documentary to satisfy your curiosity about the life of Einstein, then having his ideas about thought experiments provide an a-ha moment about how you could solve a workplace challenge). How did your curiosity foster new perspectives and additional insights?

Core Essence: Exploration. Broadening one's knowledge, thoughts, and behaviors through exploration and accumulation of novel insights and experiences.

Strength: **Fairness** (care-based, justice-based, moral reasoning) | Virtue: Justice

"Being good is easy, what is difficult is being just." - Victor Hugo

Definition: Applying notions of fairness and justice to mitigate biased thoughts and decisions about others. Treating people equally; giving everyone fair chances and equitable opportunities.

Strength in Action:

- *Simple Application:* Making sure all your kids get the same number of cookies.
- *Complex Application:* Launching a gender equality initiative within your organization that seeks to eliminate pay disparities between men and women.

Continuum of Use:

- *Underuse:* Focusing on fairness to the exclusion of all else; being disconnected from the bigger picture.
- *Optimal Use:* Providing equal opportunity for all.
- *Overuse:* Displaying inequity, bias, and partisanship; a one-sided approach to fairness.

3 Actions to Build Fairness:

- Take note of the actions and behaviors of your colleagues over the next few days, looking for circumstances where favoritism or preferential treatment are extended to certain individuals over others. Pay attention to the various ways this behavior affects those involved, including those receiving preferential treatment and those who aren't. Reflecting on what you've witnessed, look for the applicable lessons that can prevent you from making similar mistakes in the future.

- The next time you feel extremely principled about a situation, check to see if your fairness has slid to the overuse side of the spectrum. If you find you're potentially acting from a biased or one-sided perspective, intentionally seek out three opposing opinions or pieces of information to help you evaluate the scenario from a more just position.

- Surround yourself with a group of 10-year-old kids. This can be in a formal environment, like coaching a youth sports league, or in a more informal setting, such as hosting a pizza party for kids in that age range. Then, as the inevitable "that's not fair!" statement arises, act as the coach that seeks to understand the challenge being faced by the child before explaining fairness to them in an age-appropriate, applicable way. Simplifying the concept of fairness and equity will help you develop the skill within yourself.

Recommended Film: *Disney's Robin Hood.* Rob from the rich to give to the poor was Robin Hood's motto. He was outraged by the taxes Prince John unfairly assessed on the less fortunate and decided to take matters into his own hands. In the name of *fairness*, he robbed the rich, including Prince John, and gave the bounty to those with low to no means. Robin Hood didn't act alone, though; he knew the importance of *teamwork* and enlisted Little John to help with his noble shenanigans.

Robin Hood didn't always do things right, but he always did the right thing by the people of Nottingham – a notable characteristic of someone who possesses strong *leadership* skills. Leadership and teamwork are the strengths most highly correlated with fairness, and Disney's Robin Hood provides a marvelous and fun example of how these three strengths can act in conjunction with one another.

Inquiry and Reflection:

- How one practices fairness is different from person to person. What specifically does fairness mean to you? How does this definition apply to your workplace and the role you have in it? How does your definition of fairness apply to your friendships and personal relationships? If you perceive an unfair or unjust act taking place, what actions (if any) do you take? How does your definition of fairness shape who you are and what you stand for?

- Think back to a time when you felt morally conflicted. Perhaps you were expected to act in a way that compromised your personal code of conduct, or maybe you silently allowed yourself to be part of a conversation that was morally questionable. If you could go back in time, what would you do differently? Would you speak up? Perhaps, remove yourself from the situation? What actions would you take to shift the dynamic and prevent the pattern from repeating in the future?

- Looking back on a circumstance where you felt you received the short end of the stick, what was it about the situation that felt unfair or unjust? How did you react or respond at the time? If you were in that situation today, what would you do differently, if anything?

Core Essence: Just and principled. Providing equal opportunity for all.

Strength: **Forgiveness** | Virtue: Temperance

"The weak can never forgive. Forgiveness is the attribute of the strong." - Mahatma Gandhi

Definition: Accepting the wrong-doings and shortcomings of others, giving people second chances, and letting bygones be bygones.

Strength in Action:

- *Simple Application:* Quickly letting go of the irritation you feel when someone whips into a parking spot that you were patiently waiting for.
- *Complex Application:* Enlisting the help of a counselor to learn to forgive your partner for transgressions that felt personal and hurtful.

Continuum of Use:

- *Underuse:* Mercilessly blaming and condemning others for all matters of wrongdoings.
- *Optimal Use:* Releasing feelings of resentment and hurt when wronged.
- *Overuse:* Forgiving to a fault; being permissive of other's transgressions and allowing them to continue.

3 Actions to Build Forgiveness:

- Look for the good in your offenders. Frequently, the injustices felt were not intentionally or deliberately delivered and often, those who hurt us have also previously contributed to our lives in positive ways. Grab a journal and think about someone who has offended you within a professional context or environment. Putting the transgression aside, make a list of the positive interactions you've had with this person in the past, then take note of how focusing on the positives over the negatives reframes the injustice. Now, do the same in regard to a personal relationship. Consider how you can intentionally leverage this practice in the future to move forward when you've felt wronged.

- Spend the next few days watching the behaviors of others, both in professional and personal settings. Take note of what you witness when someone is hurt or offended. Evaluate if the transgression seems intentional or deliberate, or if misunderstandings play a role. Take note of whether the individuals involved addressed it on the spot or if it was allowed to fester. Look for evidence of a ripple effect, such as becoming a point of gossip or damaging additional interactions. As you consider these incidences from an outside perspective, reflect on how these acknowledgements and insights will shape your approach to forgiveness going forward.

- Strengthen your ability to forgive yourself and others using a guided forgiveness meditation. Guided meditations walk you through the process, making this meditation style easily accessible for all, including novice meditators. Guided forgiveness meditations can help you release any resentment, anger, or ill-will you're harboring and, if the transgression is especially painful, practicing this meditation for several days in a row can be incredibly powerful. A quick internet search for "guided forgiveness meditation" will provide a plethora of scripts, audios, and YouTube videos to walk you through the process.

Recommended Film: *Spider-Man 3*: An important storyline throughout the Spider-Man series surrounds the death of Peter Parker's uncle and the guilt Peter carried as a result. In *Spider-Man 3*, Peter learns who the killer was and how the events unfolded. The hatred and vengeance he had long carried suddenly began to dissipate, transcending into empathy and *forgiveness* as a new awareness of the killer's plight surfaced.

When Peter learned of the agonizing details that led up to his uncle's unintentional death and saw the genuine pain of the killer, he was filled with compassion. Almost instantly, his resentment began to melt away. Throughout Peter's character evolution, *fairness* and *leadership* are consistently displayed, the two character strengths which are most highly correlated with forgiveness.

Inquiry and Reflection:

- Think back to a situation where you forgave someone for a wrongdoing despite the fact that they didn't apologize or take responsibility for their action(s). What empowered you to forgive them? Did you leverage any of your other character strengths in the process? How did releasing the hurt help you to grow and move forward? Were there any positive lessons or personal benefits that emerged from the experience which continue to serve you today?

- Looking back on various wrongdoings you've experienced in the past, do you typically view them in black-or-white, 'either-or' terms or are you able to apply 'both-and' thinking? In other words, if a situation was negative, does that mean it was *only* negative and therefore could not contain positive aspects (either-or thinking)? Or are you able to recognize the simultaneous positives and negatives that can occur within the same event (both-and thinking)? How can you apply both-and thinking going forward to reframe transgressions before they fester into bitterness, hurt, or resentment?

- If your colleagues were asked to rate your compassion on a scale of 1 - 10, what would they say? How would your family and friends rate you? How would you rate yourself? Compassion is a key ingredient in forgiveness. This includes compassion in your interactions with others, leaving you more apt to understand their struggles and less quick to judge their actions as hurtful; compassion toward those who have hurt you so you can see their pain in addition to your own; and compassion toward yourself, empowering you to process your emotions and draw boundaries with others, while still forgiving the transgression. What actions can you take to deepen your compassion toward yourself and others?

Core Essence: Healthy release. Letting go of hurt when wronged.

Strength: **Gratitude** (thankfulness) | Virtue: Transcendence

"Some people grumble that roses have thorns; I am grateful that thorns have roses." - Alphonse Karr

Definition: An awareness of the treasured moments, gifts, and opportunities that come one's way and feeling and expressing sincere thankfulness in response.

Strength in Action:
- *Simple Application:* Thanking the person who holds open a door for you.
- *Complex Application:* Spending a few minutes each morning journaling about three things you're grateful for from the day before.

Continuum of Use:
- *Underuse:* Feeling entitled to that which you receive; demonstrating rude or ungrateful behavior.
- *Optimal Use:* Acknowledging and expressing genuine thankfulness for the goodness that surrounds you.
- *Overuse:* Leveraging gratitude as a tool to gain favor with others.

3 Actions to Build Gratitude:
- Every day for a week, write down one small thing that you normally take for granted. In a short paragraph, explore how much it means to you and expand on the value it brings which often goes unnoticed. As an example, the internet is often a small thing that is easy to take for granted, but it allows us to have video calls with family and friends, watch videos that lift our spirits, and read articles that expand our minds. At the end of the week, read your entries to heighten your awareness of the goodness that surrounds you.

- Move beyond a simple "thanks" and get detailed in your gratitude. Find three opportunities this week to replace a cursory "thank you" with expanded gratitude that elaborates on why you're so appreciative of the other person. As an example, instead of telling a friend "thanks for stopping by", let them know that you're really grateful for their wise perspective and grounded sense of humor and how their visit helped you see things more clearly.

- For six days in a row, end each day by writing down three things that occurred for which you're genuinely grateful for. Include a brief sentence for each entry detailing why it was meaningful to you and how it sparked your gratitude. On day seven, read the entries from the past six days and write a paragraph or two outlining how the exercise made you feel, taking specific note of any additional character strengths that were elevated in the process.

Recommended Film: *Groundhog Day.* Phil Conners, a local TV weatherman, isn't shy about his contempt for jobs, people, or experiences that he feels are below him. He makes no apologies for believing he's better than others and his rude, entitled behavior, which is perpetually on display, continually showcases his severe underuse of gratitude. Never a sincere "thank you" is uttered from his lips, leaving him trapped in a cycle of negativity he's created for himself. Each morning when the alarm clock sounds, it's February 1st yet again, and he can't escape the time loop he's caught in.

Initially, he uses the opportunity and lack of consequences for nefarious gain, but over time, there's nothing satisfying in these acts and he becomes desperate for a way to escape the time trap. It's not until Phil changes his approach and uses his knowledge of the town and its people to appreciate others and positively impact their lives that things begin to change. As Phil begins to genuinely acknowledge and express his *gratitude* towards those around him, his strengths of *kindness* and *love* - the two highest correlates to gratitude - are both naturally elevated, leading to profoundly positive changes in his life and relationships with others. This film is a beautiful portrayal of the wonderful changes that occur within an evolution of gratitude.

Inquiry and Reflection:

- If you were to give a speech in recognition of a lifetime achievement award, who would you thank and why? How have their roles positively impacted your life? How did your interactions with these individuals make you feel? Do they know how much you truly appreciate them? If not, what steps can you take, such as writing them a letter or paying them a visit, to genuinely express your gratitude?

- Just as a phoenix rises from the ashes, sometimes our greatest gifts spring from our deepest pain and suffering. What negative circumstances have you experienced that ultimately resulted in treasured gifts? How long did it take to recognize the benefits that were embedded in the circumstance? How do those lessons or gifts continue to serve you today? How can you show ongoing gratitude for the negative events that ultimately bring you positive results?

- Is gratitude a passive part of your life or is it something you actively seek to practice? Do you express it externally and in visible ways, or is it more of an internal feeling or emotion? Do you ever find yourself sliding on the continuum of use toward entitlement (underuse) or ingratiation (overuse)? What steps can you take to maintain a consistent, balanced gratitude practice?

Core Essence: Genuine thankfulness. Demonstrating an attitude of gratitude.

Strength: **Honesty** (authenticity, integrity) | Virtue: Courage

"To believe in something and not live it, is dishonest." - Mahatma Gandhi

Definition: Being true to oneself, both publicly and privately, and presenting oneself authentically and genuinely. Being truthful in thought and speech while taking responsibility for one's own actions and emotions.

Strength in Action:

- *Simple Application:* Acknowledging and admitting when you make a mistake.
- *Complex Application:* Delivering constructive feedback that is honest in nature, devoid of pretense, and supports the growth and development of the other.

Continuum of Use:

- *Underuse:* Appearing phony or fake; engaging in dishonest, deceitful, or insincere behavior.
- *Optimal Use:* Being authentic and sincere in thought and action.
- *Overuse:* Appearing self-righteous or morally superior; feeling more special than one is.

3 Actions to Build Honesty:

- Track how many falsehoods and white lies you express in a given day. Then, the next day, intentionally seek to reduce that number by sharing fewer falsehoods. Do this for seven days in a row, decreasing the number of white lies told each day, then compare the results from day one to day seven.
- Pulling from the core values you identified in chapter three, select a value to actively and intentionally practice every day for a week.

Evaluate how often you're true to that value and how frequently you compromise it. Determine what changes you need to make in order to live into that value with more consistency.

- Do an internet search for "quotes about honesty and integrity", then make a list of the ten quotes that resonate most deeply with you. Write a few sentences after each quote outlining the relevant lesson it holds for you and how you'll apply it going forward.

Recommended Film: *Patch Adams.* Based on a true story, Hunter "Patch" Adams' experience as a patient in the mental health system led him to the conclusion that infusing humor and compassion into patient care would produce better results than traditional medical approaches. This powerful insight captivated his soul and provided a clear path to his life's purpose, leading him to enroll in medical school. However, his personal belief system regarding the role humor should play in medicine was repeatedly called into question, nearly resulting in his permanent expulsion.

Despite the pressure to conform to traditional approaches, Adams stayed true to his beliefs, lived into his values, and demonstrated authenticity and integrity throughout his journey. His efforts were bigger than his obstacles, highlighting the *perseverance* he employed to overcome the variety of challenges that came his way. In addition, leveraging the character strength of *perspective* empowered him to see the world of patient care through a fresh lens and to share his wisdom and insights with others. Honesty is most highly correlated with perseverance and perspective, and Patch Adams is a wonderful example of the outcomes that can occur when all three strengths are combined at the optimal level of use.

Inquiry and Reflection:

- Revisiting the core values you identified in chapter three, ask yourself the following questions: How consistently are you true to yourself and your values? Do certain environments, people and/or roles empower you to live more authentically and sincerely than others? In circumstances where your thoughts, actions, and behaviors are out of alignment with your core values, what factors are contributing to the dissonance? What steps can you take to mitigate the dissonance and consistently live into your authentic self?

- Looking back on your recent interactions with others, are there ever times when you are *too* honest or when your truthfulness wades into cruelty? In these situations, what is the pretense behind your approach? Do you acknowledge and admit when mistakes are made or transgressions occur? Do you take full responsibility for your feelings and actions towards others? What steps can you take when necessity requires that you temper your honesty?

- Evaluate your actions and behaviors over the course of three days, taking note of what you do and why. Are your decisions driven by your values and personal code of conduct or are they sometimes influenced by other people's expectations? Do you find you'd rather be liked by others than principled in your approach? Do concerns over other people's interpretations of your actions influence what you do and how you do it? What steps can you take to shift the dynamic between pleasing others and living authentically and sincerely into yourself?

Core Essence: Genuine authenticity. Being true to oneself and acting authentically and sincerely towards others.

Strength: **Hope** (optimism, future mindedness, future orientation) | Virtue: Transcendence

"The pessimist sees difficulty in every opportunity. The optimist sees the opportunity in every difficulty." - Winston Churchill

Definition: Holding an optimistic view for a positive future, believing it can be brought about, and acting in ways that facilitate the desired outcome of that future.

Strength in Action:

- *Simple Application:* Feeling optimistic about an upcoming interview.
- *Complex Application:* Visualizing every detail of your upcoming business presentation in advance and envisioning yourself closing the deal.

Continuum of Use:

- *Underuse:* Possessing a pessimistic view for what the future holds; expecting negative outcomes.
- *Optimal Use:* Holding positive expectations for the future and believing your efforts influence your outcomes.
- *Overuse:* Taking an overly optimistic, unrealistic, pollyannaish view.

3 Actions to Build Hope:

- Begin each day by reading your vivid vision and anchoring yourself to the future goals you're working to achieve. To take this up a notch, record yourself reading your vivid vision and listen to it first thing when you wake in the morning and last thing before falling asleep at night. This will heighten your sense of hope and optimism for the future you're creating while deepening the neural pathways that are helping you get there.

- Take action daily on three goals that support the achievement of your vivid vision. Incremental progress in the direction of your goals and dreams not only drives hope and optimism, but also increases self-efficacy while building self-confidence.
- Reframe pessimism. When you find yourself feeling pessimistic about a given situation or scenario, immediately challenge yourself to reframe your thoughts in an optimistic way. As an example, someone who's frustrated by a newly implemented technology and feels like they'll never master it might reframe their pessimistic outlook to instead focus on the lessons they're learning which are supporting the incremental improvement they're making toward their goal.

Recommended Film: *Cast Away*. Chuck Noland, a FedEx systems analyst tasked with improving the carrier's productivity, is the lone survivor of a plane crash which leaves him stranded on a deserted island in the middle of the Pacific Ocean. During his four long years on the island, his hope and optimism are repeatedly challenged, taking the viewer on an emotional journey through the painstaking ups and downs of losing and gaining hope. Wilson, the volleyball turned best friend, becomes an icon of hope for Chuck, providing him with "someone" to talk to, hang out with, and care for.

As his relationship with Wilson deepens, a new sense of meaning fills his days, and his character strength of hope increases in response. Throughout the film, evidence of *hope* and *zest* operating in tandem are clearly evident. As Chuck's hope and optimism dwindle, so does his zest for life but as inspirational packages wash up on shore, his hope and zest simultaneously increase. One package in particular, with hand-painted wings adorning the box, becomes a beacon of hope and an anchor toward a future objective of safely, one day, delivering the package. These packages also spark a sense of *gratitude* in Chuck for the number of useful items that were shipped via FedEx and washed up on shore, Wilson among them. Zest and gratitude are most highly correlated with hope and *Cast Away* does a beautiful job of showcasing how these strengths interact and complement one another.

Inquiry and Reflection:

- Think about the people you spend the most amount of time with, be it in person or through online interactions. On a scale of 1 to 10, how optimistic are the individuals you surround yourself with? How future-oriented are they and do they take consistent action in the direction of their goals and dreams? Are there any friendships or relationships that have a pessimistic bent? How do you feel after interacting with these individuals? What can you do going forward to elevate the overall level of hope and optimism in your inner circle?

- In considering hope's continuum of use, do you typically lean more toward the optimistic end of the spectrum, the pessimistic end, or are you relatively balanced? Are there particular domains of life where you're naturally more optimistic? Are there areas where you gravitate toward a more pessimistic outlook? What lessons can you apply from the domains where you're more innately positive in order to drive hope and increase optimism in the areas that are more challenging?

- How often do you look for multiple pathways toward a given goal? Do you tend to repeatedly take the same approach with similar problems, or do you seek out unique ways to overcome obstacles? If an established approach is not working, what tactics do you use to move forward? Are you able to do so without deleterious effects on your level of hope and optimism? What steps can you take to generate more solutions (which naturally increases hope) when faced with difficult scenarios?

Core Essence: Positive expectations. Believing your efforts influence your outcomes.

Strength: **Humility** (modesty) | Virtue: Temperance

"There is nothing noble in being superior to your fellow man; true nobility is being superior to your former self." - Ernest Hemingway

Definition: Holding an accurate, uninflated view of oneself and keeping one's accomplishments and achievements in perspective, allowing them to speak for themselves.

Strength in Action:

- *Simple Application:* Allowing others to share their successes and achievements without interjecting and promoting your own.
- *Complex Application:* Conducting a 360 survey to get feedback on your leadership strengths and weaknesses from your direct reports as well as those you report to, and then modestly evaluating the insights to determine growth-oriented changes you can make in response.

Continuum of Use:

- *Underuse:* Displaying boastful, arrogant, or narcissistic behavior that inflates one's own accomplishments and achievements.
- *Optimal Use:* Holding an accurate assessment of one's abilities and limitations; allowing successes to speak for themselves.
- *Overuse:* Displaying excessively modest, self-deprecating behavior where one undervalues their contributions and worth.

3 Actions to Build Humility:

- Read a biography or watch a documentary about a successful or noteworthy individual who is also a paragon of humility. Take note of what makes the individual so humble, where their motivation comes from, and how their humility impacts both their lives as well as the lives of those around them. Look for lessons in humility that you can apply to your own life.

- Set yourself aside. Participate in a networking or business event and attempt not to talk about yourself or your accomplishments. Make others the focus of your attention by asking questions and showing genuine interest in their lives while withholding the urge to talk about your own. After the event, take note of what it felt like to focus on others and how this impacted the connections you made.

- Humbly acknowledge acts of humility in others. Be on the lookout for humble acts from colleagues or friends, then take time to acknowledge them, their humble act, and the gratitude you have for it in an equally modest way.

Recommended Film: *Dead Poet's Society.* As Welton Academy, an elite, all-male, college preparatory school, begins a fresh school year, students are caught off guard by their new English teacher, John Keating, and his unorthodox style. Creative and passionate, his humble approach toward his students puts everyone on common ground, allowing for deeply connected relationships to grow and evolve. This approach prompts his students to live life to the fullest and to seize their dreams. His students blossom and excel under his tutelage, and his *humility* prevents him from taking credit or stealing their spotlight.

Keating sees the value in each individual student and believes everyone deserves a chance to thrive and succeed, demonstrating the importance he places on *fairness*. While his style is met with significant resistance and ultimately leads to the loss of his teaching position, he continually displays a calculated level of *prudence* that empowers him to firmly make decisions that support his belief system but which he will not regret later on; a lesson he also conveys to his students. Keating's character is a wonderful illustration of an individual who leads with temperance, highlighting the character strength of humility and showcasing its interplay with its two highest correlates, prudence and fairness.

Inquiry and Reflection:

- Picture yourself attending your own funeral. As you look around the room and eavesdrop on the conversations taking place, what are others saying about you? How are they remembering you? Are they commenting on the cars you drove or the home you kept, or is the focus on who you were and what you did for others? What are the important things you want to be remembered for? What role does modesty and humility play in the legacy you want to leave after you've left this world?

- How many times in a given day or week do you actively seek to impress others? Do you portray yourself in ways that are not entirely representative of your true self? How frequently do you display an unhealthy sense of entitlement or self-importance? When you do, what are the motivations behind your actions? What steps can you take to balance confidence, ambition, and success with humility?

- Think about the most humble person you've ever personally known. How did their humility impact you? How did it impact their relationships with others? What are the various ways that their humility was on display? What lessons did you take from this individual? How can you incorporate insights from their life into yours?

Core Essence: Outward focus. Recognizing that achievement does not equate to worth.

Strength: **Humor** (playfulness) | Virtue: Transcendence

"A well-developed sense of humor is the pole that adds balance to your steps as you walk the tightrope of life." - William Arthur Ward

Definition: Seeing the lighter side of life, bringing smiles to others, infusing situations with laughter, and injecting playfulness and good cheer to produce positive emotions in oneself and others.

Strength in Action:

- *Simple Application:* Sharing something amusing to elicit a smile from a colleague.
- *Complex Application:* Intentionally looking for the humor in a trying situation and sharing it with all involved to bring levity to the moment.

Continuum of Use:

- *Underuse:* Taking an overly serious approach towards life and others.
- *Optimal Use:* Engaging in playfulness and humor, both alone and with others.
- *Overuse:* Not taking things serious enough; being overly giddy.

3 Actions to Build Humor:

- Spend a day looking for humorous moments that elicit a laugh in yourself or others. Write down a few sentences describing what sparked the funny incidents, how they impacted those involved, and how it shifted the dynamic afterwards. At the end of the day, take a few minutes to read back through your notes. Notice how humor positively impacted the day and look for lessons that you can apply going forward.

- Like anything, humor can be helpful or harmful. Lighthearted humor at the right moment can produce positive emotions that favorably enhance an interaction or event. However, mistimed or mean-spirited humor delivered at the expense of others can make a bad situation worse. Spend a day looking for negative examples of humor. Take note of why the humor was off-putting (inappropriate, poorly timed, inconsiderate, etc.) and how the misuse of humor negatively impacted the situation or people involved. At the end of the day, look for ways that the use of humor could've been adjusted to produce a positive result instead of a negative one.

- There's truth to the adage that laughter is the best medicine. Schedule a playful movie night with friends, family, or colleagues. Have the group watch a funny movie together, then openly discuss everyone's favorite parts and let the laughs continue. As an added "playful" bonus, you can play charades and have everyone act out their favorite scenes instead of just verbalizing them.

Recommended Film: *Shrek*. Donkey, who transcends from annoying outcast to Shrek's beloved friend and sidekick, embodies playfulness and humor, even in the most dire of circumstances. He uses his *humor* to brighten grim situations, bring smiles and laughter to those around him, and as a de-escalation tool when necessary. While he can sometimes overuse his humor, giving the appearance that he isn't taking things seriously enough, his humor becomes an endearing quality that those around him come to rely on. Couple this with his eternal *zest* and the way he chooses to see life as a riveting adventure filled with excitement and energy, and it's easy to see why Donkey becomes such an adored character.

In *Shrek Ever After*, the fourth film in the series, we see Donkey's personal growth continue as he begins learning to use his humor as a tool to fit into different social situations and as a means to build relationships with other characters. This becomes a wonderful example of how his signature strength of humor can be used to elevate his *social intelligence*, rounding out this trio of correlated strengths: humor, social intelligence, and zest.

Inquiry and Reflection:

- On a scale of 1 to 10, how naturally humorous are you? When is your use of humor most prevalent? When do you find it most difficult to incorporate humor? Do you deliberately use humor to relieve stress or lighten a moment? How can you elevate your use of humor in both your personal and professional roles?

- How often do you intentionally build playfulness into your schedule? What type of playful activities do you enjoy? How do you feel after taking time out to play and have fun? Do you see a connection between playfulness and feeling rejuvenated, refreshed, or generating new ideas? How can you incorporate more playfulness into your life?

- When adverse situations arise, are you able to see the lighter side or do you get mired in the seriousness of the situation? Looking back on a challenging situation, are you able to find an element of humor in what took place? How much distance or time do you typically need before you can find the lighter side in a past situation? How can you close this gap and learn to find the lighter side more quickly?

Core Essence: Lighthearted. Infusing humor and laughter to promote positive emotions.

Strength: **Judgment** (critical thinking, open-mindedness, rationality) | Virtue: Wisdom

"Too often we enjoy the comfort of opinion without the discomfort of thought." - John F. Kennedy

Definition: Examining scenarios from every angle, weighing evidence fairly and justly, and reflecting on information thoroughly to avoid rushing to conclusions. Being able to adjust one's position or change one's mind in light of presenting evidence.

Strength in Action:

- *Simple Application:* Watching two videos with opposite views on the same topic.
- *Complex Application:* Assigning an open-minded individual to play devil's advocate during a meeting and encouraging them to present obstacles and opposing viewpoints to better flush out potential solutions.

Continuum of Use:

- *Underuse:* Unreflective and disengaged from meaningful, deliberate thought.
- *Optimal Use:* Employing rationality and critical thinking when processing information and making decisions.
- *Overuse:* An unwillingness to listen to differing perspectives; maintaining a narrow-minded position.

3 Actions to Build Judgment:

- Consider a topic that you hold strong, opinionated views about. Playing devil's advocate, read three articles that express sound yet opposing viewpoints and evaluate how these additional insights shape or inform your judgments about the topic.

- Reflect on a recent disagreement you had with someone. As you replay the scenario in your mind, put yourself fully in the other person's shoes. Try to identify with the belief systems they hold and how those beliefs informed their position, then consider how these insights can help you resolve similar situations in the future.

- Think of something you've previously remained close-minded to. Perhaps it's a certain type of food you've never tried, a book you've refused to read, or a documentary you've been unwilling to consider, as examples. Flip your mindset from closed to open by embracing the experience with open arms. You may still decide it's not for you, but your decision will now be informed and educated.

Recommended Film: *Marvel's Doctor Strange.* Initially, Stephen Strange was a complicated character whose egotism and poor judgment erupted in a fiery collision that rendered his most valuable asset, his surgeon hands, useless, causing his world to implode. The loss of his hands resulted in a loss of identity, which sent him on a long, meaningful quest to become whole again. What happens in the process is an evolution of self, where Strange transcends his underuse of *judgment* to a signature strength. He becomes open-minded, learns to critically assess and evaluate all sides of a given scenario, and develops the ability to weigh evidence equally and fairly before rendering any decisions - developments that would later prove invaluable in *Avengers: Endgame.*

As Strange's judgment evolved, so did his *prudence*, which empowered him to be methodically calculated while avoiding undue and potentially harmful risks. In addition, he repeatedly leveraged the strength of *perspective* to make sense of the tornado of chaos surrounding him and to wisely counsel his fellow Avengers on how to take action. Perspective and prudence are the highest correlated strengths with judgment and Dr. Strange's character provides a wonderful example of how these strengths can work together to elevate the virtues of wisdom and temperance.

Inquiry and Reflection:

- Learning to approach challenges with an open mind that considers all sides of an issue has been shown to improve decision making. Reflecting on a recent challenge, did you operate from preconceived notions and assumptions or did you seek additional information and broaden your ability to critically assess the issue at hand? How will you intentionally expand your ability to think critically in the future?

- Groupthink is a phenomenon that occurs when members within a group prioritize harmony and conformity above all else, eliminating space for dissent or alternative thought processes. The end result is poor decision making that is devoid of critical thinking and lacks meaningful analysis. Think about a time or scenario where you experienced or witnessed groupthink. If you were to go back in time, how would you address or alter the situation? What could you have said or done to change the dynamic or outcome?

- Think of a recent occurrence when you changed your mind on a particular issue in response to new or additional information. What caused this shift in thinking for you? Did you seek out additional information? Did you listen to a viewpoint you hadn't previously considered?

Core Essence: Rational analysis. Examining all sides of a situation or subject and evaluating all perspectives equally and fairly.

Strength: **Kindness** (generosity, nurturance, care, compassion, altruism) | Virtue: Humanity

"No act of kindness, no matter how small, is ever wasted." - AESOP

Definition: Performing good deeds, doing favors, and helping others without reciprocal expectations.

Strength in Action:

- *Simple Application:* Opening the door for someone.
- *Complex Application:* Recognizing a decline in a neighbor's health and mowing their lawn for them.

Continuum of Use:

- *Underuse:* Displaying an attitude of indifference, selfishness, or stinginess; lacking compassion and caring for others.
- *Optimal Use:* Doing for others without expecting anything in return; demonstrating care, compassion, and niceness.
- *Overuse:* Inserting oneself in an intrusive or meddlesome manner where kindness becomes overbearing.

3 Actions to Build Kindness:

- Perform three random acts of kindness, one for a stranger, one for a colleague or coworker, and one for a friend or family member. Then, reflect on how each of these acts made you feel, paying attention to the differences you experience depending on who your kindness is directed towards.
- Make a list of seven different ways that you can extend compassion and kindness to yourself, then practice one each day over the next week.

Take note of the ways that kindness towards yourself reduces stress and anxiety while promoting optimism.

- Watch *Pay it Forward* with a group of friends or colleagues, and then challenge the group to act in kind, spreading generous, altruistic, or compassionate acts of kindness to the surrounding community. Get together again a week later to collectively discuss the experiences everyone had in the process and to explore the positive impact it had on all involved.

Recommended Film: *Pay it Forward*. On the first day of class, a group of students are challenged by their social studies teacher to think of a project that would have the ability and potential to positively change the world. Trevor, one of the students, takes the task to heart and creates a "pay it forward" project where one person performs an act of kindness for three others, then those three people each pay-it-forward to three more, and before you know it, genuine acts of kindness are being spread far and wide.

As the film unfolds, *kindness* touches hearts and changes lives in unexpected ways, allowing the characters to see the positive even in the most negative of circumstances. The success of Trevor's project was rooted in supporting others through *teamwork*, while *gratitude* from both the givers and the receivers became a consistent theme throughout the movie. This film beautifully illustrates how kindness, and its highest correlated strengths of gratitude and teamwork, can truly change the world.

Inquiry and Reflection:

- Looking back over the last week, list various acts of kindness you performed for others. This can include small acts, such as holding doors open for others; larger acts, such as rescuing a coworker whose car broke down and needed a ride to work; and anything in between. How does reflecting on the kindness you extended to others make you feel? How did those acts affect your interaction or engagement with those individuals?

- In what ways are you generous with your time? Do you mentor others? Do you make yourself available when a friend needs to chat? Do you volunteer for local organizations? What emotions do you experience when you gift your time to others?

- If coworkers were asked if you're a kind person, what would their responses be? What would the response be if the same question was posed to friends and family? Are there times, circumstances, or environments where you are less kind? What steps can you take to increase your awareness in this area?

Core Essence: Niceness. Doing for others without expectation.

Strength: **Leadership** | Virtue: Justice

"Leadership is the art of getting someone else to do something you want done, because he wants to do it." - Dwight D. Eisenhower

Definition: Influencing, inspiring, and encouraging a group of individuals to achieve common tasks and goals while maintaining positive, productive relations within the group.

Strength in Action:
- *Simple Application:* Organizing happy hour for a group of friends.
- *Complex Application:* Soliciting meaningful feedback from all employees, crafting a unifying vision based on their input, and inspiring the organization to continually live into the vision.

Continuum of Use:
- *Underuse:* Demonstrating an acquiescent and compliant approach.
- *Optimal Use:* Positively motivating, inspiring, and influencing others to take action on common goals.
- *Overuse:* Taking a tyrannical approach that exerts absolute power.

3 Actions to Build Leadership:
- Read a biography about a leader whom you admire and respect. Keep a journal detailing the various lessons you resonate with and how they can be adapted and applied to your life.
- Search the internet for leadership quotes and make a list of seven quotes you most identify with. As examples, you may choose quotes that inspire you, those that challenge you to improve, or quotes which serve as reminders of the type of leader you want to be. Print the list,

then deliberately practice the essence of each quote, one per day, over the next week.
- Take an online leadership course through a service like Coursera to further develop your leadership strength while gaining a deeper understanding of how to motivate and inspire others toward achieving common goals.

Recommended Film: *Invictus*. This beautiful story of leadership and unification illustrates the power and importance of influence, inspiration, and encouragement in the pursuit of meaningful goals. Nelson Mandela, recognizing the enormous post-Apartheid challenges that were facing his nation, sought to address the racial divisions between black and white South Africans, fearing that if he did nothing, violence would ensue.

In a moment of insight - a common occurrence for self-aware leaders - Mandela saw a unique opportunity for race unification in the most unusual setting, a rugby match. Realizing that sports could be a conduit to unite and inspire the country, Mandela approached François Pienaar, the captain of the country's rugby team, and the two embarked on a shared *leadership* journey to take the team and the country to new heights. Their *teamwork*, which was rooted in a shared desire to create equality and *fairness* for all South Africans, showcases the incredibly positive changes that can occur when leadership is partnered with its two highest correlates, fairness and teamwork.

Inquiry and Reflection:
- There are times when it's necessary to lead, and times when even the leader must follow. How adept are you at recognizing when you need to step up and lead, versus when it's time to fall back, support, and follow? Do you find one role to be more natural than the other? If your colleagues were asked if you're a good leader, what would they say? How would they respond to being asked if you're a good follower?

What actions can you take to achieve appropriate balance in these roles?

- Do you recognize and acknowledge signature strengths in those around you? Do you actively help others see how their strengths can be leveraged to achieve their goals? What specific steps can you take to tap into other's strengths and inspire them to action? How can you empower others to see their own strengths as valuable assets to be utilized on a daily basis?

- Think about the best leader you've ever worked for or with. What qualities did this person possess that made them stand out? What noteworthy actions did they take? How did your interactions with them make you feel? What tone did their leadership style set among the group or organization? If you were to describe this person in five words, what would those words be? How can you incorporate these words into your personal leadership philosophy?

Core Essence: Inspirational influence. Motivating others to take action on common goals.

Strength: **Love** (loving others, being loved by others) | Virtue: Humanity

"Hatred cannot coexist with love and kindness. It dissipates when supplanted with thoughts of love and compassion." - from the Dhammapada

Definition: Valuing close, connected relationships with others. This can include love for those who care for you, love for those whom you care for, and reciprocal relationships where love and care are mutually shared.

Strength in Action:

- *Simple Application:* Withholding advice and simply listening to a friend who needs a supportive, non-judgmental ear.
- *Complex Application:* Intentionally seeking to ensure that you have five times as many positive interactions in your relationships as negative.

Continuum of Use:

- *Underuse:* Emotional isolation that keeps you distanced and disconnected from others.
- *Optimal Use:* Reciprocal love and support that promotes feelings of safety and security in connection with others.
- *Overuse:* Emotional promiscuity that rapidly, frequently, and indiscriminately establishes relationships with others.

3 Actions to Build Love:

- Strengthen your feelings of connection to yourself and others using a Loving-Kindness meditation, also known as a "metta" meditation. This flexible form of meditation is accessible to all and does not require previous meditation experience. A quick internet search for "Loving-

Kindness meditation" will produce a host of scripts, audios, and YouTube videos to walk you through the process. Just choose the style that resonates most with you, find a comfortable place to sit, and enjoy the experience.

- Grab a piece of paper and draw a line down the center. In the left-hand column, make a list of a loved one's favorite things. This can include activities, food, drinks, movies, books, etc. On the right, make a list of your own favorite things. Next, identify areas of overlap, then plan a special surprise that incorporates those shared favorite things. Afterwards, explore the emotions you each experienced in the process and how this exercise contributed to the connection between you.

- Spend a day intentionally looking for opportunities to perform spontaneous acts that spread love toward those around you. This can be as simple as an encouraging word, a listening ear, or a meaningful embrace, and can be expressed towards family, friends, colleagues, and even strangers. At the end of the day, take note of the experiences you had and how they shaped your mood and emotions.

Recommended Film: *The Blind Side*. "Big Mike", as he's affectionately known, is a homeless teenager who spent years bouncing through the foster care system after being abandoned by his drug-addicted mother at age seven. While attending high school, a fellow student from a well-off family recognized the challenges Mike was facing and befriended him, leading to the family's awareness of Mike's plight.

Leigh Anne, the classmate's mom, extended her *love*, care and support to Mike, offering this practical stranger meals, clothes, and a place to sleep. Over time, the bond grew, and this stranger became a valued member of the family, eventually leading to his adoption, a college education, and an ensuing career in the NFL. Leigh Anne's *kindness* toward Mike, combined with the *gratitude* she held for who he was and the positive role he played in her family's life, showcased the transformative power that love has when it acts in concert with its highest correlated strengths of gratitude and kindness.

Inquiry and Reflection:

- Think about someone you share a close, personal bond with but whom you don't see as often as you'd like. Looking back to the last interaction you shared, what is it about your connection that makes this person so special to you? How does thinking about this person make you feel? What words come to mind when you think about your relationship with them? In what specific ways do you two express your love and caring for one another?

- Expressing loving kindness isn't restricted to personal relationships; genuine warmth can also be spread to strangers. Think about your daily interactions with random people. In what ways do you express love, compassion, and support for or towards strangers? What types of responses do you receive in return? How do positive interactions with strangers shape your mood and/or contribute to your day?

- How does the character strength of love show up for you at work and in professional settings? Are you warm and supportive towards those around you? Do you feel supported by others? Do you feel there is an equal balance of give and take? If not, are you typically on the giving end or the receiving end? What actions can you take to enhance the connections you have with others professionally?

Core Essence: Genuine warmth. Giving and receiving love in connection with others.

Strength: **Love of Learning** (knowledge acquisition) | Virtue: Wisdom

"The pleasures arising from thinking and learning will make us think and learn all the more." - Aristotle

Definition: Systematically building one's skillsets and/or adding to their body of knowledge to master particular topics or subjects. This can be done informally, as a personal endeavor, or through formal education. This is related to Curiosity but moves beyond mere interest in a subject, allowing for new knowledge to be acquired and leveraged.

Strength in Action:

- *Simple Application:* Reading three articles or blog posts on the same subject.
- *Complex Application:* Reading three books and taking a certification course in a given area of interest to improve or expand your skillset and elevate your knowledge base.

Continuum of Use:

- *Underuse:* Demonstrating complacency or a lack of interest in deepening one's knowledge and understanding.
- *Optimal Use:* Experiencing positive feelings and emotions surrounding educational pursuits that build knowledge and skills.
- *Overuse:* Becoming a know-it-all who appears arrogant and uses their depth and breadth of knowledge in unhelpful or unhealthy ways.

3 Actions to Build Love of Learning:

- Join (or start) a book club, exploring the book's subject matter at a deeper level and engaging in conversation and discussion with others.

- Take a class to learn more about an area that interests you or to further develop and enhance a skill that you'd like to improve upon.
- Many museums now offer virtual tours that allow their exhibits to be explored from the comfort of your own home. Choose a museum whose subject matter interests you, then spend an afternoon strolling through their virtual halls and learning about the various installations.

Recommended Film: *Harry Potter and the Philosopher's Stone.* Hermione Granger embodies a love of learning with every ounce of her soul. Prior to arriving at Hogwarts, she had already immersed herself in the upcoming education by memorizing the majority of her textbooks in advance. Her passion for mastering the wide swath of subjects covered at the wizarding academy is a focal point in her storyline, though admittedly, her love of learning is initially overused, leaving her labeled as a know-it-all.

However, as the series repeatedly illustrates, her love of learning and the knowledge acquired as a result, empowers her to come to the rescue of her friends and fellow classmates, who lack the same level of wizarding knowledge and know-how. Coupled with her *love of learning*, Hermione also displays an on-going sense of *curiosity* that fuels her explorations and discoveries, while regularly taking time to acknowledge the skilled performance of others (*appreciation of beauty & excellence*), especially those professors who showcase admirable wizarding prowess, such as Professor McGonagall. As Hermione's character illustrates, when love of learning is combined with its most highly correlated strengths of curiosity and appreciation of beauty and excellence, the acquired knowledge can be applied in meaningful, transformative ways.

Inquiry and Reflection:
- Thinking back to the last class, course, or seminar you attended, what motivated you to make that selection? How did you apply the newly

acquired knowledge, and what benefits were reaped for yourself and/or others as a result?

- Considering the continuum of use, think of a time when you slid to the complacency end of the spectrum. What was the end result? Now consider a situation where you gravitated toward overuse, what was the impact? What specific strategies can you employ to maintain optimal balance?

- Think back to a time when you intentionally leveraged learning to overcome a particular problem or challenge. What was the scenario and how did your learning-centric approach impact the situation and/or those around you?

Core Essence: Knowledge expansion. Continually and systematically deepening one's knowledge with excitement and fervor.

Strength: Perseverance (industriousness, persistence) | Virtue: Courage

"With ordinary talent and extraordinary perseverance, all things are attainable." - Sir Thomas Fowell Buxton

Definition: Pushing persistently through obstacles to finish what one starts. Taking pleasure in the completion of tasks and the achievement of goals.

Strength in Action:

- *Simple Application:* Setting a target of 25 outbound, business-generating phone calls per day and not stopping until all 25 have been completed.
- *Complex Application:* Creating a multi-year learning agenda that consists of multiple courses in the pursuit of a particular degree or certification and proceeding consistently and continually until the final objective is achieved.

Continuum of Use:

- *Underuse:* Feeling helpless or giving up; failing to believe that effort and persistence produce results.
- *Optimal Use:* Persistently pursuing goals while overcoming obstacles or challenges that arise in the process.
- *Overuse:* Obsessively pursuing a given path or goal, regardless of whether it's meaningful or fits within a larger vision.

3 Actions to Build Perseverance:

- Gamify your approach by setting incremental improvement targets, tracking your daily progress, and seeking to improve your results every day. As an example, let's say you want to write a book. Set a goal of writing 300 words on the first day, then increase by ten words a day (tracking it as you go along) until flow kicks in and your daily habit of writing streams naturally and with less forced effort.

- Perseverance and consistency go hand-in-hand so don't break the chain. Print out a calendar, post it in an obvious place that can't be ignored, and mark each day with a big green checkmark when you complete the task or practice the behavior you've committed to. As an example, if your goal is to perpetually expand your industry knowledge, your task may be to read industry-related books or articles for 30-minutes per day. Once the task is complete, you celebrate with a big green checkmark.

- Watch a film that showcases perseverance and resilience in action, then take note of the lessons presented and how they can be incorporated into your life and situation. Some films to consider include the *Rocky* series, *Shawshank Redemption*, *Finding Nemo*, *The Pursuit of Happyness*, and *Cast Away*.

Recommended Film: *The Karate Kid*. This film provides a wonderful illustration of how persistence can both be taught and learned. When Daniel, the main character, finds himself being bullied and abused on a regular basis, his first inclination was to give up and give in to the daily obstacles that presented themselves. However, his perspective changed when he witnessed the martial arts skills of Mr. Miyagi.

Daniel saw this skillset as a means to overcome his challenges and enlisted Mr. Miyagi as a mentor, though what would follow was not what Daniel expected. From washing and waxing rows of cars, to painting miles of fence, to sanding expansive areas of wooden decking, Daniel found it difficult to see the relevance of these actions, but the beautiful theme that emerged was one of *perseverance*, resilience, and grit. In addition, Mr. Miyagi consistently reinforced the importance of being disciplined in one's emotions, thoughts, and actions - a lesson in *self-regulation* that was essential to Daniel's growth and development. Mr. Miyagi also emphasized lessons on *honesty* and the importance of genuinely evaluating and taking responsibility for one's feelings and actions, showcasing the powerful combination that exists when perseverance is combined with its two highest correlated character strengths, self-regulation and honesty.

Inquiry and Reflection:

- Do you have clarity on your big picture goals and the incremental tasks and subgoals required to bring larger goals to fruition? Do you prioritize goal-directed tasks and activities over non-essential activities? Do your daily and weekly efforts directly support your vision and future self? When challenges and obstacles present themselves, do you focus on the importance of pushing through to achieve your larger goals? If not, how could adopting this mindset drive your persistence?

- Make a list of the obstacles that regularly disrupt your progress and inhibit your persistence. What patterns or themes emerge from your list? Are there certain circumstances, people, or environments that commonly derail your efforts? What changes can you make to optimally use persistence and overcome the obstacles that stand between you and your goals?

- Think of an unsupportive habit you currently hold and would like to eliminate, perhaps one that is out of alignment with your future self. How can you intentionally use persistence to overcome the habit? What benefits will be achieved when the habit no longer has its hold on you? How will this contribute to your ability to push through fears and obstacles and achieve your goals?

Core Essence: Grit. Putting in continual effort to overcome obstacles and achieve goals.

Strength: **Perspective** (integrating additional viewpoints) | Virtue: Wisdom

"The optimist sees the donut, the pessimist sees the hole." - Oscar Wilde

Definition: Being able to look at the bigger picture, consider other points of view, and offer sage advice and wise counsel to others. The ability to look at situations in ways that help make sense for oneself and for others. Demonstrating wisdom.

Strength in Action:

- *Simple Application:* Sharing an apt quote with someone that meaningfully speaks to a particular challenge they're facing.
- *Complex Application:* Seeking out multiple viewpoints from various stakeholders to ensure that all sides of an issue can be addressed before a final decision is rendered.

Continuum of Use:

- *Underuse:* Appearing shallow or thoughtless; trapped in habitual patterns of thought that fail to consider new or differing information.
- *Optimal Use:* Holding a bigger picture perspective that empowers one to see the forest *and* the trees.
- *Overuse:* Forcing a certain perspective on others in an overbearing or forceful fashion.

3 Actions to Build Perspective:

- Read a biography or watch a documentary about a wise individual who consistently embraces multiple viewpoints while demonstrating a bigger picture perspective. Take notes on the insights that arise for you.

- Connect with a friend or mentor who regularly draws on their knowledge and experience in ways that helps others. Engage in a conversation to learn more about how their wisdom surfaces, what intentional efforts they put into the process, and the reciprocal benefits they receive as a result.
- Volunteer your time mentoring a child or young adult in your community. Practice listening to the perspectives they share surrounding their challenges, then draw on your knowledge and experience to provide wisdom and counsel.

Recommended Film: *Star Wars: Episode V - The Empire Strikes Back.* Yoda, with his sage advice and infinite wisdom, is the embodiment of *perspective*. He provides Luke with deep insights and wise counsel, continually drawing from his vast experience with life, the force, and the powerful pull of the dark side. He repeatedly challenges Luke to see the bigger picture in a variety of scenarios, though does so with patience, discernment, and grace. Yoda understands the importance of prudently providing caution, insight, and awareness without forcing his knowledge or perspectives on others, demonstrating balanced, optimal use of this powerful strength.

While Episode V results in Luke ultimately choosing a path that was discouraged by his wise mentor, Yoda recognizes that wisdom can be shared but never forced. This is one of many examples throughout the series where Yoda evaluates scenarios from every angle, weighing all evidence, and demonstrating the equally important role that *judgment* plays in his life. His consistent sensitivity to the motivations of others and his ability to see in them what they have yet to recognize in themselves is an illustration of the *social intelligence* he also brings to the equation. The character strengths of social intelligence and judgment are the most highly correlated with perspective and Yoda's character provides an empowering example of how these three strengths can commingle to heighten the virtue of wisdom.

Inquiry and Reflection:

- Think of a recent disagreement you had with someone close to you. We're you able to step back from the content of the argument and see the person? Or did the topic of the disagreement become the focal point, causing you to lose sight of the bigger picture? How would you approach this situation differently if it were to occur today?

- Are there certain scenarios or environments in which you're more likely to evaluate the bigger picture and consider multiple perspectives? Are there topics or situations where you are less likely to incorporate multiple views and more apt to respond from habit? How can you apply the lessons from the former to the latter?

- Thinking back on someone (past or present) who served as a role model in your life, what qualities did this person exhibit that made them such a great support system? What aspects of their approach, personality, or skills would you like to adopt or develop?

Core Essence: The bigger picture. Seeing the forest *and* the trees.

Strength: **Prudence** | Virtue: Temperance

"Prudence is the knowledge of things to be sought, and those to be shunned." - Cicero

Definition: Being mindful of one's choices and the implications they hold for the future. Being careful not to say or do things that one may later come to regret.

Strength in Action:

- *Simple Application:* Packing a lunch to take to work so you're not tempted to grab unhealthy, fast food.
- *Complex Application:* Writing a 90-day goal plan in support of your vision, then making daily choices that support the achievement of your plan.

Continuum of Use:

- *Underuse:* Making decisions based on immediate gratification without consideration for future implications.
- *Optimal Use:* Demonstrating wise caution and discernment; weighing risks against benefits.
- *Overuse:* Appearing overly cautious or excessively self-restrained; an unwillingness to take balanced risks.

3 Actions to Build Prudence:

- Prudence plays a role in knowing which character strength(s) to leverage in various situations. Spend a full day intentionally utilizing your prudence to evaluate different strengths to be used in varying circumstances. Perhaps you need heightened judgment before weighing in on a workplace challenge, or maybe you need to elevate your hope in order to push through a tough obstacle. At the end of the day, take note of how your intentional use of prudence enhanced your additional strengths.

- With your next important decision, take time to apply long-term thinking and imagine the implications and outcomes this decision will produce one, five and ten years down the road. Evaluate how a longer-term perspective filtered through your vivid vision impacts your decision making in the present. Determine if there are certain types of decisions that you should consistently evaluate in this way.

- Connect with a colleague whom you'd describe as a pinnacle of patience and prudence and ask for their insights and advice on how to be more prudent in your everyday life. Be prepared with specific questions, demonstrating the priority you place on this strength and the respect you have for their command of it. Find out how they maintain prudent decision making when faced with options that seem immediately obvious or appealing. Ask them to share stories about the positive benefits they've experienced as a result of their prudence.

Recommended Film: *Driving Miss Daisy*. In this heartwarming film about a wealthy, Jewish widow and an African American chauffeur, the recurrent theme of *prudence*, a strength shared by both characters, is foundational to the bond that forges their deeply meaningful 25-year friendship. 72-year-old Miss Daisy, after crashing her car into a neighbor's yard, recognizes the long-term implications of continuing to get behind the wheel and, albeit with some initial reluctance, accepts the idea of allowing a chauffeur to drive her. Slowly over time, she builds a close relationship with Hoke, the patient and perceptive driver, whose prudence is consistently on display throughout the film.

While Miss Daisy was initially focused on their differences, their time spent together made her realize they had more in common than she originally thought, demonstrating the *judgment* and critical thinking required for her to change her mind when presented with more information. This acknowledgement also elevates her *humility*, which empowered her to connect with Hoke on a more personal level and to stop thinking of herself as more special than she is. Judgment and humility are the highest correlated strengths with prudence, and this film gives a wonderful illustration of how these three strengths can work together to deepen relationships and build flourishing bonds.

Inquiry and Reflection:

- When you think of prudence, what definition comes to mind? On a scale of 1 to 10, where 1 reflects prudence as a negative trait and 10 portrays it as positive, how do you personally rank prudence? Do you view prudent people as overly cautious or do you view them as balanced and wise? What is your explanation for why prudence is so often displayed as an unfavorable trait in movie characters? How can you incorporate the positive aspects of prudence into your daily life without shifting into underuse or overuse?

- Prudent people (those operating at the point of optimal use) balance long-term goals with present-day decision making. They consider the future implications of their actions and are willing to sacrifice immediate gratification for the benefit of their long-term plans. Do you maintain a balanced approach between long-term goals and short-term gains? Are you able to recognize when a decision will have short-term benefits but be detrimental to the long game? What steps can you take to maintain focus on the bigger picture?

- Prudence involves making conscientious choices about actions and behaviors. How do your daily actions and behaviors support your goals? Do you take consistent action in the direction of your vision and dreams? Are your daily activities supporting your future self and who you are becoming? What steps can you take to intentionally increase your prudence and be more mindful of the implications your choices hold for your future?

Core Essence: Cautious wisdom. Applying practical wisdom to weigh risks against benefits.

Strength: **Self-Regulation** (self-control) | Virtue: Temperance

"Today I will do what others won't, so tomorrow I can accomplish what others can't." - Jerry Rice

Definition: Showing control over one's thoughts, impulses, emotions, and actions; demonstrating discipline in the pursuit of goals.

Strength in Action:

- *Simple Application:* Getting out of bed when the alarm sounds and resisting the urge to hit the snooze button.
- *Complex Application:* Taking action for 90-days straight to replace a habit of procrastination with a habit of proactivity.

Continuum of Use:

- *Underuse:* Giving into impulses, thoughts, and actions that are immediately gratifying; engaging in self-indulgent behavior.
- *Optimal Use:* Managing one's vices; regulating actions, behaviors, and thoughts in support of long-term benefits.
- *Overuse:* Inhibiting one's thoughts, emotions, and actions to a fault; being overly controlled.

3 Actions to Build Self-Regulation:

- Practice mindfulness. Research has shown that mindfulness enhances self-regulation, empowering the practitioner to focus their thoughts while reducing internal chatter. Start with an easy process, such as closing your eyes and following your breath for 3-minutes, feeling the sensation of the breath move throughout your body as you take long, deep inhales followed by slow, deliberate exhales. Engaging in this practice twice daily will increase your self-regulation.

- Enlist the help of an accountability partner. Having a trusted ally to hold you accountable to your goals and objectives is a proven method for building and enhancing self-regulation. Creating a reciprocal relationship where each other's visions are known, goals are shared, and tasks and objectives are tracked and measured, helps drive self-regulation while enhancing the rate at which goal achievement occurs.

- Identify an unsupportive behavior that is preventing you from achieving your goals. Write the behavior on a piece of paper then monitor yourself for the next three days. Each time you catch yourself in the act, think about the steps that led up to the behavior. Identifying the triggers that preempt the unsupportive behavior empowers you to replace it with a more supportive alternative. As an example, if you notice procrastination occurs in your workday after a bout of frustration, start taking a short walk after frustrating incidents so you can return to your work with a fresh mind and a renewed spirit.

Recommended Film: *Twilight.* As a vampire in love with a human, Edward Cullen epitomizes self-regulation. While it's not without its challenges, he makes a commitment to live the vampire equivalent of a vegetarian lifestyle, regulating his instinct and desire to consume human blood. On a continual basis, he showcases self-control in managing his impulses, emotions, and appetites, separating himself from Bella, his human love interest, when temptations become too overwhelming to control.

Over the course of five films, Edward's *self-regulation* is in full force, as is his *perseverance,* which supports and propels his commitment to protect Bella from other vampires at all costs, no matter the obstacles. His life with Bella is a true adventure that leaves him feeling alive and energized, demonstrating his character strength of *zest* and the role it plays in enhancing their connection and romance. Perseverance and zest are the most highly correlated strengths with self-regulation and throughout the

Twilight Saga, countless examples of the intersection of these strengths are on display.

Inquiry and Reflection:

- Think back to an unsupportive behavior you once struggled with but have since overcome. What was the behavior and how did it negatively impact your life? What brought you to the conclusion that this behavior had to be altered? How were you able to increase your self-control and eliminate or reduce the behavior? Which additional strengths enhanced your self-regulation and helped you overcome the unsupportive behavior or habit?

- Looking back on a significant accomplishment that required a substantial amount of time to complete, what motivated the self-regulation to see the goal through to the end? What strategies did you employ to keep vices at bay and ensure continued progress? How can the lessons from your past successes apply to future long-term goals?

- Self-control is a transferable skill. In other words, developing self-control in one area of life positively enhances your self-regulation in other domains of life. Choosing an area of life (health, career, relationships, etc.), where can you intentionally demonstrate discipline to increase your overall self-regulation? Some examples include engaging in a daily exercise regimen, committing 30-minutes per day to read professionally relevant articles, spending thirty technology- and distraction-free minutes each day in conversation with a loved one. Is there an area of life where it's more difficult for you to keep unsupportive habits in check? How can you take the success of self-regulation in an easier domain of life and apply it to an area where you struggle?

Core Essence: Balanced control. Demonstrating discipline in thoughts, emotions, and actions.

Strength: **Social Intelligence** (emotional intelligence, personal intelligence) | Virtue: Humanity

"When people talk, listen completely. Most people never listen."
- Ernest Hemingway

Definition: Knowing how to adapt and fit into different social situations while possessing insights and awareness into the motives and feelings of others and oneself. Understanding what motivates people and makes them tick.

Strength in Action:

- *Simple Application:* Noticing the sad tone in a friend's voice and offering supportive comfort and a listening ear.
- *Complex Application:* Navigating the emotions and motivations of different department heads as you seek to unify corporate efforts toward a common goal.

Continuum of Use:

- *Underuse:* Being obtuse or clueless about one's surroundings; lacking insight or awareness.
- *Optimal Use:* Recognizing situational factors, motives, and feelings, then acting in accordance with said insights.
- *Overuse:* Over analyzing what is sensed about others and taking inappropriate action in response.

3 Actions to Build Social Intelligence:

- The next time a loved one shares a frustration, listen with intentional empathy, withholding the urge to give advice or rebut their position. Focus intently on actively listening to their thoughts, emotions, and sentiments without simultaneously formulating a response in your mind. Afterwards, connect with how it felt to listen empathically as opposed to communicating actively, and take note of the impact it had on the interaction.

- Revisiting a recent conflict you had with somebody, look for at least one positive element that was present in the other person's feelings or motivations. Try to identify what informed their perspective and drove their position. Reflect on how these insights, and your deeper understanding of them, can better support your interactions going forward.

- Timing is a critical aspect of social intelligence. As an example, consider the coworker who tells a funny joke - at the most inappropriate time. Spend the day taking note of the timing displayed by others. Look for examples where timing was off and disrupted the environment, as well as positive examples such as when the perfect timing of an empathic question moves a situation forward. Consider how your insights and awareness on timing will impact your approach going forward.

Recommended Film: *Hitch*. In this film, the title character is a professional "date doctor" who possesses an elevated *social intelligence* that includes a natural ability to read women, understand what they're thinking and feeling, and connect with them in a meaningfully, genuine way. He uses this signature strength as a tool to help sincere men, who are less adept at connecting with women, find love. In his role as a relationship coach, his uncanny ability to read a social situation and understand peoples' feelings and motives enables him to share spot-on advice and wise counsel to his clients, a *perspective* that allows them to see dating through a fresh lens and overcome the challenges they face in interacting with their love interests.

In addition, his *leadership* strength can be seen in the way he coaches others to get clear on their vision and goals, then motivates and inspires them to grow and evolve in pursuit of those goals. *Hitch* is not only a touching and funny film, but it's also a wonderful example of how the strength of social intelligence is enhanced when partnered with its two highest correlated strengths, perspective and leadership.

Inquiry and Reflection:

- Are there situations where you commonly misread or misinterpret the actions and behaviors of others? What leads to your incorrect assumptions? What steps can you take to double-check your assumptions before taking action?

- Ask a close friend or loved one for honest feedback regarding how well you listen and how supported they feel when sharing with you. Listen actively to their feedback and reflect on the words and feelings they share. Introspect on why they feel the way they do and connect with any emotions you're having in response. What changes, if any, will you make in response to this feedback?

- How attuned are you to your own feelings and emotions? When you start to get angry or frustrated, are you able to introspect on why or are your responses reactive? How do you respond to others when you disagree with their ideas or opinions? How much time do you spend in thought, reflecting on your own feelings and motivations? How would a deeper understanding of yourself allow you to connect differently with others?

Core Essence: Attuned. Reads other people then takes informed, appropriate action in response.

Strength: **Spirituality** (purpose, meaning, faith, religiousness) | Virtue: Transcendence

"Life is never made unbearable by circumstances, but only by lack of meaning and purpose." - Viktor Frankl

Definition: Holding coherent beliefs about the higher purpose of the universe, the meaning of life, and one's place within both. Having personal practices and beliefs surrounding the universe or a higher power that shapes one's conduct while providing comfort.

Strength in Action:

- *Simple Application:* Feeling an immense sense of meaning while volunteering for a favorite organization.
- *Complex Application:* Devoting two hours each day towards activities that aim to support and develop your purpose in life.

Continuum of Use:

- *Underuse:* Meaningless efforts that feel empty and inconsequential.
- *Optimal Use:* Connecting with the larger meaning and purpose in one's life.
- *Overuse:* Engaging in fanaticism; taking beliefs to an unsupportive, unhealthy level.

3 Actions to Build Spirituality:

- Read a biography or watch a documentary about a spiritual person whom you admire and respect. Capture any ideas or insights that resonate with you along the way and journal about them as you go. Review your notes, then choose three action items to implement in your own life.

- Choose an item or artifact that represents your spiritual beliefs and write a paragraph or two about why this item reflects your spirituality. As an example, let's say an individual's spirituality revolves around extending kindness and compassion to others knowing that everyone is on their own path to growth and development. They may choose a butterfly as an artifact that encompasses their beliefs about spirituality, growth, and their purpose in life to facilitate the transformation of others in their own time.

- Develop a daily meditation or prayer practice to deepen your self-awareness, enhance your mindfulness, and connect with your higher purpose. If you're new to mindfulness, consider reading *Wherever You Go, There You Are: Mindfulness Meditation in Everyday Life* by Jon Kabat-Zinn, Ph.D. This easy-to-read book is composed of short chapters that perfectly illustrate the spirit and essence of mindfulness, providing a roadmap to develop one's personal practice.

Recommended Film: *The Way*. This beautiful film captures the powerful essence of spiritual evolution, following the journeys of multiple individuals who are walking the Camino de Santiago (also known as The Way of Saint James) in search of greater meaning in their lives. For Dr. Thomas Avery, this was an unexpected journey. Initially, he set out on the Camino to retrieve his son's remains, who had sadly perished in a storm while walking through the Pyrenees. However, as an expression of his grief, and in an attempt to better understand his son as well as honor the journey his son was on, Tom decides to embark on the historical pilgrimage himself, finishing what his son had started.

Along his journey, Tom meets other pilgrims, each yearning to understand the bigger purpose in their lives, eventually forming an unlikely quartet who, after countless adventures that evoke tears of sadness and laughter, form a lifelong bond. It's through these experiences that Tom comes to understand his son, appreciate the differences they shared, develop his own sense of *spirituality*, and find new meaning and purpose in life. While it took time for Tom to let his guard down and learn the lessons that life was presenting, as he did, his *gratitude* for the people and experiences put in his path and his *hope* for a more meaningful future began to grow and expand, demonstrating the strength that exists when spirituality is amplified by its two highest correlates, gratitude and hope.

Inquiry and Reflection:

- Spirituality means different things to different people. What is your personal definition of spirituality? What regular practices do you engage in that support your spirituality? How do your spiritual beliefs surrounding meaning and purpose shape your conduct and interactions with others? How can you deepen your spiritual practices and enhance your meaning and purpose in common, everyday activities?

- If you knew your last day on earth would be exactly one year from today, how would you spend your time? Who would you spend it with? What legacy would you seek to leave behind? What do your answers tell you about what gives your life purpose, meaning, and joy?

- Think back to a time when you experienced a major shift or transformation in your life. What role did your purpose or meaning play in this transformation? How did your spirituality shape your response? Did the shift occur gradually over time or was there a catalyst moment that propelled the transformation? How did this shift affect or enhance your ongoing spiritual practices?

Core Essence: Clarity of purpose. Seeing one's fit in the bigger design.

Strength: **Teamwork** (citizenship, social responsibility, loyalty) | Virtue: Justice

"Coming together is the beginning. Keeping together is progress. Working together is success." - Henry Ford

Definition: Being a loyal member of a group or team who pulls one's own weight and does their fair share to support group initiatives. Prioritizes efforts for the good of the group over personal gain.

Strength in Action:

- *Simple Application:* Soliciting feedback from a coworker on a group project that you're spearheading.
- *Complex Application:* Identifying individuals with varying signature strengths to create a well-rounded team to design, develop, and launch a new corporate initiative.

Continuum of Use:

- *Underuse:* Displaying a self-centered and selfish approach that leaves no space for the contributions of others.
- *Optimal Use:* Collaborating with others and participating in group efforts while performing one's individual fair share.
- *Overuse:* Relying too heavily on teamwork and becoming dependent on others to an unhealthy extreme.

3 Actions to Build Teamwork:

- Volunteer at a local community organization where your unique combination of strengths and talents can be leveraged in a team environment to help the organization achieve their mission and goals.

- Spend one week deliberately making efforts to encourage and foster increased morale among a team you're an active part of. Keep track of the approaches you try and the results they garner. Seek to have more positive interactions than negative and to help others do the same. At the end of the week, ask a teammate for feedback on your efforts so you can continue to grow and evolve as a team facilitator.

- Coordinate a group outing to an escape room. These challenging environments can only be overcome with efficient teamwork, communication, and collaboration. Time pressure associated with the 60-minute countdown clock will reveal more about team dynamics in one fast hour than a month of teamwork in a traditional setting. Reserve time after the event to celebrate areas where communication and teamwork were strong, as well as to discuss any areas for growth.

Recommended Film: *Avengers: Infinity War* and *Avengers: Endgame*. While movies that showcase *teamwork* are plentiful, a wonderful and recent example can be found in the last two Avenger's films. Each of the characters brought their individual strengths to the table, set aside any differences they had with one another, and unified their efforts to achieve their common goal: defeat Thanos and save humankind.

These films illustrate the importance of team collaboration, effective communication, group problem solving, cooperation, and sacrificing individual achievement for the success of the whole. Countless examples of *leadership* are also on display, such as when T'Challa motivates and coordinates the Wakandan military to join forces with the Avengers, or when Tony Stark sacrifices himself for the good of the mission. *Kindness* also ripples throughout the films and can be seen in the way Tony Stark cares for Peter Parker, or in the good deeds that each of the superheroes performed on a regular basis. Leadership and kindness are the strengths most highly correlated with teamwork, and evidence of their combined mightiness can be seen repeatedly throughout these two films.

Inquiry and Reflection:

- Make a list of the different areas in life where you're part of a team. This may include personal, professional, extracurricular, or volunteer endeavors. When participating in these various team efforts, how often do you focus on the group versus yourself? Does your verbiage reflect "we" statements or "I" statements? Does your self-talk reflect a team approach or an individualistic mindset? Do you notice a difference in your approach based on the setting you're in? How can you take the strengths you display in one area and apply them to another?

- Think back to an event or occasion when you put your own accomplishments on hold to prioritize the efforts of your group or team. Did you have any hesitation in doing so or was it an easy choice? What was the outcome of your decision to prioritize the team over your individual efforts? What effects did it have on team morale? What effects did it have on your personal relationships with your teammates? How can you apply these lessons going forward?

- Effective teamwork directly impacts a group's ability to succeed, regardless of whether it's within a personal or a professional environment. How effective are you at teamwork and collective problem solving within your family unit? How about with your circle of friends? Do you find you approach teamwork differently when it's personal versus professional?

Core Essence: Collaborative. Participating in, and supporting, group efforts.

Strength: **Zest** (vitality, vigor, energy) | Virtue: Courage

"If you have zest and enthusiasm you attract zest and enthusiasm. Life does give back in kind." - Normal Vincent Peale

Definition: Living life to the fullest with exuberance, excitement, and energy. Approaching life as an adventure to be lived whole-heartedly and with a sense of vitality and aliveness.

Strength in Action:

- *Simple Application:* Decidedly taking an upbeat stance during a business meeting.
- *Complex Application:* Designing an employee engagement program that infuses colleagues and coworkers with a morning boost of excitement and energy to kickstart the day.

Continuum of Use:

- *Underuse:* Lethargic, sedentary behavior; boredom and passivity in approach to events and affairs.
- *Optimal Use:* Enthusiasm for life that energizes oneself and others; intentionally infusing vitality and excitement.
- *Overuse:* Hyperactivity or unfettered eagerness that becomes off-putting and unappealing to others.

3 Actions to Build Zest:

- Take a break from your current environment and get physical. Whether you go for a hike surrounded by the beauty of nature, take a workout class at the local gym, or head out for an evening walk around the neighborhood, moving your body leads to increased levels of vitality and zest.

- Create a playlist of energizing, upbeat songs. Any time you need a pick me up, get up on your feet, hit play, and let the music move you.
- Own the morning and you own the day. Create a morning routine that feeds your soul and sets the stage for an enthusiastic, productive day.

Recommended Film: *Hook*. In this wonderful film, Peter Banning (formerly Peter Pan) is a grown man who has completely lost the enthusiasm and excitement he once held for life. He's a stressed out, workaholic lawyer who is successful by corporate standards, but is equally oblivious to the reality that his personal relationships are deeply strained. Peter lacks the vitality and energy that contributes to healthy relationships, life satisfaction, and a meaningful and engaged life. That is, until he's reminded of who he once was and begins to reconnect with the *zestful* memories of his past.

As Peter returns to his roots of treating life as an adventure to be lived whole-heartedly, his *hope* for a better, brighter future begins to expand and his sense of *curiosity* and exploration are dramatically amplified. The evolution of Peter's character illustrates the remarkable changes that can occur in one's life when zest is combined with its highest correlated strengths, hope and curiosity.

Inquiry and Reflection:

- In what settings do you feel most energized and excited? Is your enthusiasm amplified by anything in particular, such as music, certain people, or specific activities? When you're having an off day, what elements can you deliberately incorporate to reinvigorate your energy and enthusiasm?
- How do you approach mundane tasks and projects? Do you undertake humdrum chores in an uninspiring way? Do you find the fun in mundane tasks and infuse them with energy and enthusiasm? What

deliberate steps can you take to make your next chore an enthusiastic experience?

- How do you manage your energy and enthusiasm on a daily basis? Do you have a morning routine that sets the tone for your day? Do you have a regular bedtime that ensures you get a full night's sleep? Do you incorporate exercise or physical movement into your daily routine? What steps can you take to foster and better manage your energy on an ongoing and continual basis?

Core Essence: Exuberance and excitement. Approaching life with intentional enthusiasm.

REFERENCES

chapter one:

1. Wheatley, M. J. (2006). *Leadership and the new science: Discovering order in a chaotic world* (3rd ed.). San Francisco, CA: Berrett-Koehler Publishers, Inc. (p. 24)

2. Kotter, J. P. (2012). Change management. Accelerate! *Harvard Business Review, 90*(11), 44-58

3. Boyatzis, R. E., Smith, M. L., Van Oosten, E., & Woolford, L. (2013). Developing resonant leaders through emotional intelligence, vision and coaching. *Organizational Dynamics, 42*(1), 17-24.

4. Senge, P. M. (2006). *The fifth discipline: The art & practice of the learning organization.* New York, NY: Currency. (p. 215)

5 - Clearfield, C., & Tilcsik, A. (2019). *Meltdown: Why our systems fail and what we can do about it.* London, United Kingdom: Atlantic Books.

6. Meadows, D. H. (2015). *Thinking in systems: A primer.* White River Junction, VT: Chelsea Green Publishing.

7. Carpenter, S. (2020). *Work the system: The simple mechanics of making more and working less.* Austin, TX: River Grove Books.

8. Bryan, Judith F, & Locke, Edwin A. (1967). GOAL SETTING AS A MEANS OF INCREASING MOTIVATION. *Journal of Applied Psychology,51*(3), 274-277.

chapter two:

1. Block, P. (2018). *Community: The structure of belonging.* Oakland, CA: Berrett-Koehler Publishers.

2. Ibid.

3. Kouzes, J. M., & Posner, B. Z. (2017). *The leadership challenge: How to make extraordinary things happen in organizations* (6th ed.). Hoboken, NJ: John Wiley & Sons, Inc.

4. Harrington, H. J., & Voehl, F. (2016). Chapter 1, 5 Whys. In *The Innovation Tools Handbook, Volume 2: Evolutionary and Improvement Tools that Every Innovator Must Know* (pp. 1-10). Boca Raton, FL: CRC Press.

5. Serrat O. (2017) The Five Whys Technique. In: Knowledge Solutions. *Springer,* Singapore. https://doi.org/10.1007/978-981-10-0983-9_32

6. Williams, P., & Denney, J. (2004). *How to be like Walt: Capturing the Disney magic every day of your life* (pp. 3-15). Deerfield Beach, FL: Health Communications.

7   Helmstetter, S. (2014). *The Power of Neuroplasticity* (p. 14). Gulf Breeze, FL: Park Avenue Press

8   Passarelli, A. M., (2015). Vision-based coaching: Optimizing resources for leader development. *Frontiers in Psychology, 6*, 412

9   Locke, E., & Latham, G. (2006). New Directions in Goal-Setting Theory. *Current Directions in Psychological Science, 15*(5), 265-268, p.265

10 Stavros, J. M., Torres, C., & Cooperrider, D. L. (2018). *Conversations Worth Having: Using Appreciative Inquiry to Fuel Productive and Meaningful Engagement* (p. 22). Oakland, CA: Berrett-Koehler, Incorporated

11 Peterson, C., & Seligman, M. (2004). *Character strengths and virtues: A handbook and classification*. Washington, DC: American Psychological Association; Oxford University Press.

12 Niemiec, R. M. (2018). Spotlight on Hope. *Character strengths interventions: A field guide for practitioners*. Boston, MA: Hogrefe

13 Niemiec, R. M., & Wedding, D. (2014). *Positive psychology at the movies: Using films to build character strengths and well-being* (p. 284). Boston, MA: Hogrefe

14 Ibid.

15 Boyatzis, R. E., Erochford, K., & Taylor, S. N., (2015). The Role of the Positive and Negative Emotional Attractors in Vision and Shared Vision: Toward Effective Leadership, Relationships and Engagement. *Frontiers in Psychology, 6*, 670.

16 Ibid.

17 Ibid.

18 Fredrickson, B., & Stafford, T. (2004). What good are positive emotions? *Psychologist, 17*(6), 331.

19 Ashby, F., Isen, A., & Turken, U. (1999). A Neuropsychological Theory of Positive Affect and Its Influence on Cognition. *Psychological Review, 106*(3), 529-550.

20 Boyatzis, R. E., Erochford, K., & Taylor, S. N., (2015). The Role of the Positive and Negative Emotional Attractors in Vision and Shared Vision: Toward Effective Leadership, Relationships and Engagement. *Frontiers in Psychology, 6*, 670.

21 Ibid.

22 Passarelli, A. M., (2015). Vision-based coaching: Optimizing resources for leader development. *Frontiers in Psychology, 6*, 412, p. 4

23 Stavros, J. M., Torres, C., & Cooperrider, D. L. (2018). *Conversations Worth Having: Using Appreciative Inquiry to Fuel Productive and Meaningful Engagement.* Oakland, CA: Berrett-Koehler, Incorporated, p. 107

24 Kirschenbaum, D.S., Ordman, A.M., Tomarken, A.J. et al. Effects of differential self-monitoring and level of mastery on sports performance: Brain power bowling. *Cognitive Therapy and Research 6*, 335–342 (1982). https://doi.org/10.1007/BF01173581

25 Santilli, S., Ginevra, M., Sgaramella, T., Nota, L., Ferrari, L., & Soresi, S. (2015). Design My Future: An Instrument to Assess Future Orientation and Resilience. *Journal of Career Assessment. 25*(2) 281-295.

26 Ibid.

27 Locke, E., & Latham, G. (2002). Building a Practically Useful Theory of Goal Setting and Task Motivation. *American Psychologist, 57*(9), 705-717.

28 Dweck, C. S. (2006). *Mindset: The new psychology of success* (p. 7). New York, NY: Ballantine Books a division of Random House Inc.

29 Ibid.

chapter three:

1 Johnson & Johnson Staff Writer. (2019, January 22). 133 Years of Innovative Credo-Driven Decisions That Have Made Johnson & Johnson the Healthcare Leader It Is Today. Retrieved November 10, 2020, from https://www.jnj.com/our-heritage/timeline-of-johnson-johnson-credo-driven-decisions

2 Johnson & Johnson Staff Writer. (n.d.). Our Credo. Retrieved November 10, 2020, from https://www.jnj.com/credo/

3 Ibid.

4 De Witte, M. (2019, August 14). Why 'Find your passion!' may be bad advice. Retrieved November 10, 2020, from https://news.stanford.edu/2018/06/18/find-passion-may-bad-advice/

5 Fotuhi, M., & Antoniades, C. B. (2014). *Boost your brain: The new art and science behind enhanced brain performance.* San Francisco, CA: HarperOne.

6 Association for Psychological Science. (2014, May 12). Having a sense of purpose may add years to your life, study finds. Retrieved November 10, 2020, from https://medicalxpress.com/news/2014-05-purpose-years-life.html

7 Leider, R. (2015). *The power of purpose: Find meaning, live longer, better.* Oakland, CA: Berrett-Koehler.

8 Ibid.

9   Boyatzis, R., Erochford, K., & Taylor, S., (2015). The Role of the Positive and Negative Emotional Attractors in Vision and Shared Vision: Toward Effective Leadership, Relationships and Engagement. *Frontiers in Psychology, 6*, 670.

chapter four:

1   Senge, P. M. (2006). *The fifth discipline: The art & practice of the learning organization* (p. 166). New York, NY: Currency.

2   Block, P. (2018). *Community: The structure of belonging*. Oakland, CA: Berrett-Koehler Publishers.

3   Dr. Geil Browning, https://www.inc.com/geil-browning/personal-reflection-get-started-with-these-5-questions.html

4   Senge, P. M. (2006). *The fifth discipline: The art & practice of the learning organization* (p. 171). New York, NY: Currency.

chapter five:

1   Boyatzis, R. E., Smith, M., & Oosten, E. V. (2019). *Helping people change: Coaching with compassion for lifelong learning and growth* (p. 40). Boston, MA: Harvard Business Review Press.

2   Peterson, C., & Seligman, M. (2004). *Character strengths and virtues: A handbook and classification*. Washington, DC: American Psychological Association; Oxford University Press.

3   Niemiec, R. M. (2018). *Character strengths interventions: A field guide for practitioners*. Boston, MA: Hogrefe.

4   Ibid.

5   Fredrickson, B. L. (2001). The Role of Positive Emotions in Positive Psychology. *The American Psychologist, 56*(3), 218-226.

6   Fredrickson, Barbara L, Mancuso, Roberta A, Branigan, Christine, & Tugade, Michele M. (2000). The Undoing Effect of Positive Emotions. *Motivation and Emotion, 24*(4), 237-258.

7   Tugade, Michele M, & Fredrickson, Barbara L. (2004). Resilient Individuals Use Positive Emotions to Bounce Back From Negative Emotional Experiences. *Journal of Personality and Social Psychology, 86*(2), 320-333.

8   Niemiec, R. M. (2018). *Character strengths interventions: A field guide for practitioners*. Boston, MA: Hogrefe.

9   Csikszentmihalyi, M. (2009). *Flow: The psychology of optimal experience* (pp. 49 - 53). New York, NY: Harper Row.

10 University of Penn. (n.d.). PERMA™ Theory of Well-Being and PERMA™ Workshops. Retrieved November 13, 2020, from https://ppc.sas.upenn.edu/learn-more/perma-theory-well-being-and-perma-workshops

11 Wagner, L., Gander, F., Proyer, R.T. *et al.* Character Strengths and PERMA: Investigating the Relationships of Character Strengths with a Multidimensional Framework of Well-Being. *Applied Research Quality Life* **15,** 307–328 (2020).

12 Can we improve our Physical Health by Altering our Social Networks? https://journals.sagepub.com/doi/10.1111/j.1745-6924.2009.01141.x

13 University of Penn. (n.d.). PERMA™ Theory of Well-Being and PERMA™ Workshops. Retrieved November 13, 2020, from https://ppc.sas.upenn.edu/learn-more/perma-theory-well-being-and-perma-workshops

14 Ibid.

15 Niemiec, R. M. (2018). *Character strengths interventions: A field guide for practitioners.* Boston, MA: Hogrefe.

16 Wagner, L., Gander, F., Proyer, R.T. *et al.* Character Strengths and PERMA: Investigating the Relationships of Character Strengths with a Multidimensional Framework of Well-Being. *Applied Research Quality Life 15*, 307–328 (2020).

17 Ibid.

18 Ibid.

19 University of Penn. (n.d.). PERMA™ Theory of Well-Being and PERMA™ Workshops. Retrieved November 13, 2020, from https://ppc.sas.upenn.edu/learn-more/perma-theory-well-being-and-perma-workshops

20 Niemiec, R. M. (2018). *Character strengths interventions: A field guide for practitioners.* Boston, MA: Hogrefe.

21 Wagner, L., Gander, F., Proyer, R.T. *et al.* Character Strengths and PERMA: Investigating the Relationships of Character Strengths with a Multidimensional Framework of Well-Being. *Applied Research Quality Life 15,* 307–328 (2020).

22 University of Penn. (n.d.). PERMA™ Theory of Well-Being and PERMA™ Workshops. Retrieved November 13, 2020, from https://ppc.sas.upenn.edu/learn-more/perma-theory-well-being-and-perma-workshops

23 Seligman, M. E. (2013). *Flourish: A visionary new understanding of happiness and well-being.* New York, NY: Atria.

24 Niemiec, R. M. (2018). *Character strengths interventions: A field guide for practitioners.* Boston, MA: Hogrefe.

25 Wagner, L., Gander, F., Proyer, R.T. et al. Character Strengths and PERMA: Investigating the Relationships of Character Strengths with a Multidimensional Framework of Well-Being. *Applied Research Quality Life 15,* 307–328 (2020).

26 Niemiec, R. M. (2018). *Character strengths interventions: A field guide for practitioners* (p. 2). Boston, MA: Hogrefe.

27 Wagner, L., Gander, F., Proyer, R.T. et al. Character Strengths and PERMA: Investigating the Relationships of Character Strengths with a Multidimensional Framework of Well-Being. *Applied Research Quality Life 15,* 307–328 (2020).

28 Holt, S., Marques, J. Empathy in Leadership: Appropriate or Misplaced? An Empirical Study on a Topic that is Asking for Attention. *Journal of Business Ethics 105,* 95–105 (2012). https://doi.org/10.1007/s10551-011-0951-5

29 Goleman, D. (2006). *Emotional intelligence: Why it can matter more than IQ.* New York, NY: Bantam Books.

30 Peterson, C., & Seligman, M. (2004). *Character strengths and virtues: A handbook and classification.* Washington, DC: American Psychological Association; Oxford University Press.

chapter six:

1 Duhigg, C. (2014). *The power of habit: Why we do what we do in life and business.* St. Louis, MO: Turtleback Books.

2 Ibid.

3 Galla, Brian M, & Duckworth, Angela L. (2015). More than resisting temptation: Beneficial habits mediate the relationship between self-control and positive life outcomes. *Journal of Personality and Social Psychology, 109*(3), 508-525.

4 Wemm, Stephanie E, & Wulfert, Edelgard. (2017). Effects of Acute Stress on Decision Making. *Applied Psychophysiology and Biofeedback, 42*(1), 1-12.

5 Reay, Trish, Golden-Biddle, Karen, & Germann, Kathy. (2006). Legitimizing a New Role: Small Wins and Microprocesses of Change. *Academy of Management Journal, 49*(5), 977-998.

6 Goldsmith, M., & Reiter, M. (2016). *Triggers.* New York, NY: Random House.

7 Hardy, B. (2019). *Willpower doesn't work: Discover the hidden keys to success.* New York, NY: Hatchette Book Group.

8 Meadows, D. H. (2015). *Thinking in systems: A primer.* White River Junction, VT: Chelsea Green Publishing.

9   Duhigg, C. (2014). *The power of habit: Why we do what we do in life and business*. St. Louis, MO: Turtleback Books.

10 Clear, J. (2018). *Atomic habits: An easy & proven way to build good habits & break bad ones*. New York, NY: AVERY an imprint of Penguin Random House.

11 Ibid.

12 Duhigg, C. (2014). *The power of habit: Why we do what we do in life and business*. St. Louis, MO: Turtleback Books.

13 Fogg, B. J. (2019). *Tiny habits: The small changes that change everything*. London, UK: Virgin Books.

14 Rubin, G. C. (2015). *Better than before: what I learned about making and breaking habits--to sleep more, quit sugar, procrastinate less, and generally build a happier life*. Anchor Canada.

15 Tang, Yi-Yuan, Holzel, Britta K, & Posner, Michael I. (2015). The neuroscience of mindfulness meditation. *Nature Reviews. Neuroscience, 16*(5),

16 Ibid.

17 Ibid.

18 Duckworth, A. L., & Seligman, M. E. (2005). Self-discipline outdoes IQ in predicting academic performance of adolescents. *Psychological science, 16*(12), 939–944. https://doi.org/10.1111/j.1467-9280.2005.01641.x

19 H. Maejima et al., (2018). Exercise and low-level GABAA receptor inhibition modulate locomotor activity and the expression of BDNF accompanied by changes in epigenetic regulation in the hippocampus. *Neuroscience Letters*, 685:18–23, 2018.

20 Van Der Werf, Ysbrand D, Altena, Ellemarije, Schoonheim, Menno M, Sanz-Arigita, Ernesto J, Vis, José C, De Rijke, Wim, & Van Someren, Eus J W. (2009). Sleep benefits subsequent hippocampal functioning. *Nature Neuroscience, 12*(2), 122-123.

21 Nere, A., Hashmi, A., Cirelli, C., & Tononi, G. (2013). Sleep-Dependent Synaptic Down-Selection (I): Modeling the Benefits of Sleep on Memory Consolidation and Integration. *Frontiers in Neurology, 4*, 143.

22 Boyatzis, R. E., Smith, M., & Oosten, E. V. (2019). *Helping people change: Coaching with compassion for lifelong learning and growth*. Boston, MA: Harvard Business Review Press.

23 Margol, E. G. (2019, August 29). How to Utilize the Neuroscience of Gratitude. https://tier1performance.com/what-neuroscience-studies-say-about-gratitude/.

chapter seven:

1. Clear, J. (2018). *Atomic habits: An easy & proven way to build good habits & break bad ones.* New York, NY: AVERY an imprint of Penguin Random House.

chapter eight:

1. Locke, Edwin A, & Latham, Gary P. (2002). Building a practically useful theory of goal setting and task motivation. A 35-year odyssey. *The American Psychologist, 57*(9), 705-717.

2. Bryan, Judith F, & Locke, Edwin A. (1967). GOAL SETTING AS A MEANS OF INCREASING MOTIVATION. *Journal of Applied Psychology, 51*(3), 274-277.

3. Latham, G.P., Locke, E.A. and Fassina, N.E. (2005). The High Performance Cycle: Standing the Test of Time. In *Psychological Management of Individual Performance* (eds P. Herriot and S. Sonnentag). doi:10.1002/0470013419.ch10

4. Phillips, Jean M, & Gully, Stanley M. (1997). Role of Goal Orientation, Ability, Need for Achievement, and Locus of Control in the Self-Efficacy and Goal-Setting Process. *Journal of Applied Psychology, 82*(5), 792-802.

5. Bandura, A. & Cervone, D. (1983). Self-evaluative and self-efficacy mechanisms governing the motivational effects of goal systems. *Journal of Personality and Social Psychology, 45*(5), 1017-1028.

6. Latham, G.P., Locke, E.A. and Fassina, N.E. (2005). The High Performance Cycle: Standing the Test of Time. In *Psychological Management of Individual Performance* (eds P. Herriot and S. Sonnentag). doi:10.1002/0470013419.ch10

7. Ibid.

8. Phillips, J.M., & Gully, S.M., (1997). Role of Goal Orientation, Ability, Need for Achievement, and Locus of Control in the Self-Efficacy and Goal-Setting Process. *Journal of Applied Psychology, 82*(5), 792-802.

9. Bandura, A., & Cervone, Daniel. (1983). Self-evaluative and self-efficacy mechanisms governing the motivational effects of goal systems. *Journal of Personality and Social Psychology, 45*(5), 1017-1028.

10. Bryan, Judith F, & Locke, Edwin A. (1967). GOAL SETTING AS A MEANS OF INCREASING MOTIVATION. *Journal of Applied Psychology, 51*(3), 274-277.

11. Bandura, A. (1977). Self-efficacy: Toward a unifying theory of behavioral change. *Psychological Review, 84,* 191-215.

12. Dominican University of California - Dr. Gail Matthews Study: citation - Gardner, Sarah and Albee, Dave, "Study focuses on strategies for achieving

goals, resolutions" (2015). *Press Releases*. 266.
https://scholar.dominican.edu/news-releases/266

13 Ibid.

14 Bryan, Judith F, & Locke, Edwin A. (1967). GOAL SETTING AS A MEANS OF INCREASING MOTIVATION. *Journal of Applied Psychology, 51*(3), 274-277.

15 Locke, Edwin A, & Latham, Gary P. (2002). Building a practically useful theory of goal setting and task motivation. A 35-year odyssey. *The American Psychologist, 57*(9), 705-717.

16 Latham, G.P., Locke, E.A. and Fassina, N.E. (2005). The High Performance Cycle: Standing the Test of Time. In *Psychological Management of Individual Performance* (eds P. Herriot and S. Sonnentag). doi:10.1002/0470013419.ch10

17 Collins, J., & Porras, J. I. (2004). *Built to last: Successful habits of visionary companies.* London, UK: Random House Business Books.

18 Martin, Bruce, McNally, Jeffrey, & Taggar, Simon. (2016). Determining the Importance of Self-Evaluation on the Goal-Performance Effect in Goal Setting: Primary Findings. *Canadian Journal of Behavioural Science, 48*(2), 91-100.

chapter ten:

1 Aigbedion, A. E., 2016. Understanding the Neural Basis of Intention. *Current Research in Neuroscience, 6*: 23-27.

2 Dominican University of California - Dr. Gail Matthews Study: citation - Gardner, Sarah and Albee, Dave, "Study focuses on strategies for achieving goals, resolutions" (2015). *Press Releases*. 266.
https://scholar.dominican.edu/news-releases/266

3 Goldsmith, M., & Reiter, M. (2016). *Triggers.* New York, NY: Random House.

4 Brown, S. L., & Vaughan, C. C. (2010). *Play: How it shapes the brain, opens the imagination, and invigorates the soul.* New York, NY: Avery.

5 Ibid.

appendix:

1 - Peterson, C., & Seligman, M. (2004). *Character strengths and virtues: A handbook and classification.* Washington, DC: American Psychological Association; Oxford University Press.

2 - Ibid.

3 - Ibid.

Acknowledgments

*"If I have seen further than others,
it is by standing on the shoulders of giants."*

- Isaac Newton

This book has been a labor of love, but it humbly rests on the shoulders of those who contributed to my growth and development, both personally and indirectly. To all, I am deeply thankful.

To Jan Burdick, whose time on this planet was far too short, thank you for demonstrating what strong, effective, female leadership looks like and for giving me the first leadership opportunity of my career. You planted a seed that has long continued to grow and blossom and I will forever be thankful for you.

To Dr. Christina Wilson, no words can adequately convey the immense value received from your selfless mentorship or the dear appreciation I hold for you. Your lessons continue to shape and influence me on a daily basis, and I am eternally grateful for the role you've played in my life.

To my Gonzaga family, especially Dr. Michael Carey, Dr. Deborah Hedderly, Dr. Adrian Popa, Dr. Joe Albert, and Meghan Semmens. Your unending support made space for my goals and dreams to take shape and materialize on the pages of this book. I am STRENGTHENED because of the role each of you played in my journey.

To the small handful of incredibly horrible bosses who I worked for or with over the years, thank you for igniting my passion for ethical, effective leadership. Your lessons on how *not* to lead inspired my passion for positively impacting the leadership equation. I'm a better leader because of you.

And lastly, to those whom I've never met but whose research, efforts, and teachings have informed my personal and professional development, my sincerest appreciation for making my journey possible. Peter Block, Richard Boyatzis, Brené Brown, David Cooperrider, Mihaly Csikszentmihalyi, Carol Dweck, BJ Fogg, Barbara Fredrickson, Marshall Goldsmith, Daniel Goleman, Benjamin Hardy, Jeff Hiatt, James Kouzes, Gary Latham, Edward Locke, Ryan Niemiec, Christopher Peterson, Barry Posner, Martin Seligman, and Peter Senge.

About the Author

"Become the change you wish to see in the world."

- Mahatma Gandhi

Leadership examples are everywhere. They exist across a broad continuum, ranging from exemplary models of success to morale-busting blueprints of what *not* to do. They can teach one how to inspire others to greatness, or they can outline the perfect path to a painful demise.

Over her 30-year career (twenty-years in corporate America and the last ten years as a business coach and consultant), Laura W. Miner has experienced both ends of the leadership spectrum. Her early experiences sparked her love and passion for identifying the positive patterns that led to flourishing cultures and collective goal achievement. But over time, she grew equally intrigued by the negative behaviors that invariably led to toxic work environments and organizational implosions.

Laura spent the bulk of her corporate career as a Sales Manager in the technologies field – a role that required her to wear the hats of consultant, trainer, facilitator, and presenter. She worked with thousands of businesses of varying sizes, helping them to design better business practices, increase their revenues, and create heightened customer experiences. In this role, she witnessed a wide array of leadership styles and developed an increasing sensitivity toward the direct impact leaders have on their followers.

In 2009, when she made the transition from employee to entrepreneur, she naively believed that all negative leadership experiences would be in the rearview mirror. Surely, as a consultant, Laura would only encounter positive environments where rainbows and unicorns adorned every office space.

Then, it happened - the straw that broke the unicorn's back. A succession of three contracts where she grew increasingly frustrated with, and saddened over, the repetition of a common pattern.

She'd be hired to work with a sales and marketing team who were facing business challenges, only to discover that the underlying issues originated with the organizational culture and the executive teams' philosophies toward leadership. Though the trickle-down effect seemed obvious from her vantage point, leadership insights from a sales consultant were rarely, if ever, welcomed.

This led to a period of deep introspection where she realized that, for far too many years, she'd been part of the problem instead of the solution. She worked with companies to drive revenue through sales and marketing tactics all the while ignoring the toxic cultures that prioritized profits over people. Motivated by her desire to help companies and executives at a much deeper level, she elected to scale back her career and pursue a formal education in the leadership sciences.

She now holds a bachelor's degree in psychology with an emphasis in organizational psychology from University of Colorado Denver, and a master's degree in organizational leadership from Gonzaga University with an emphasis in change leadership.

She works with emerging and established leaders, as well as organizational teams, helping them to identify and embrace their strengths, adapt their behaviors to achieve their goals, and break down the barriers that prevent success. Her growth-minded approach supports the development of leaders who foster growth and achievement in others while simultaneously creating a positive environment that improves employee morale and increases productivity.

Laura is available for speaking events, corporate training seminars, leadership development coaching, and organizational consulting. You can learn more about her personal leadership philosophy by visiting **http://lwm.link/philosophy** and you can reach her via email at **hello@laurawminer.com**.

Share Your Opinion

"When you learn, teach. When you get, give."

- Maya Angelou

Have time to share your opinion? Leave a review for STRENGTHENED by visiting **http://lwm.link/review**. Taking a few minutes to pen your thoughts goes a long way toward helping me get the word out about my book.

With love and appreciation,

Laura W. Miner

Photo by Ati Grinspun Photography

You are not here merely **to make a living.** You are here in order to **enable the world** to live more amply, with greater vision, with a finer spirit of **hope and achievement.** You are here to **enrich the world, and** you impoverish yourself if you forget the errand.

Woodrow Wilson

Made in United States
Orlando, FL
05 January 2022

13063696R00167